▶ **Mobile Media Making in an Age of Smartphones**

DOI: 10.1057/9781137469816.0001

Other Palgrave Pivot titles

Isabel Harbaugh: Smallholders and the Non-Farm Transition in Latin America

Daniel A. Wagner: Learning and Education in Developing Countries: Research and Policy for the Post-2015 UN Development Goals

Murat Ustaoğlu and Ahmet İncekara: Islamic Finance Alternatives for Emerging Economies: Empirical Evidence from Turkey.

Laurent Bibard: Sexuality and Globalization: An Introduction to a Phenomenology of Sexualities

Thorsten Botz-Bornstein and Noreen Abdullah-Khan: The Veil in Kuwait: Gender, Fashion, Identity

Vasilis Kostakis and Michel Bauwens: Network Society and Future Scenarios for a Collaborative Economy

Tom Watson (editor): Eastern European Perspectives on the Development of Public Relations: Other Voices

Erik Paul: Australia as US Client State: The Geopolitics of De-Democratization and Insecurity

Floyd Weatherspoon: African-American Males and the U.S. Justice System of Marginalization: A National Tragedy

Mark Axelrod: No Symbols Where None Intended: Literary Essays from Laclos to Beckett

Paul M. W. Hackett: Facet Theory and the Mapping Sentence: Evolving Philosophy, Use and Application

Irwin Wall: France Votes: The Election of François Hollande

David J. Staley: Brain, Mind and Internet: A Deep History and Future

Georgiy Voloshin: The European Union's Normative Power in Central Asia: Promoting Values and Defending Interests

Shane McCorristine: William Corder and the Red Barn Murder: Journeys of the Criminal Body

Catherine Blair: Securing Pension Provision: The Challenge of Reforming the Age of Entitlement

Zarlasht M. Razeq: UNDP's Engagement with the Private Sector, 1994–2011

James Martin: Drugs on the Dark Net: How Cryptomarkets Are Transforming the Global Trade in Illicit Drugs

Shin Yamashiro: American Sea Literature: Seascapes, Beach Narratives, and Underwater Explorations

Sudershan Goel, Barbara A. Sims, and Ravi Sodhi: Domestic Violence Laws in the United States and India: A Systematic Comparison of Backgrounds and Implications

DOI: 10.1057/9781137469816.0001

palgrave▸pivot

Mobile Media Making in an Age of Smartphones

Edited by

Marsha Berry
Royal Melbourne Institute of Technology, Australia

and

Max Schleser
Massey University, New Zealand

DOI: 10.1057/9781137469816.0001

MOBILE MEDIA MAKING IN AN AGE OF SMARTPHONES
Copyright © Marsha Berry and Max Schleser, 2014.

First published in 2014 by
PALGRAVE MACMILLAN®
in the United States—a division of St. Martin's Press LLC,
175 Fifth Avenue, New York, NY 10010.

Where this book is distributed in the UK, Europe and the rest of the world,
this is by Palgrave Macmillan, a division of Macmillan Publishers Limited,
registered in England, company number 785998, of Houndmills,
Basingstoke, Hampshire RG21 6XS.

Palgrave Macmillan is the global academic imprint of the above companies
and has companies and representatives throughout the world.

Palgrave® and Macmillan® are registered trademarks in the United States,
the United Kingdom, Europe and other countries

ISBN: 978-1-137-46982-3 EPUB
ISBN: 978-1-137-46981-6 PDF
ISBN: 978-1-137-48265-5 Hardback

Library of Congress Cataloging-in-Publication Data

Mobile media making in an age of smartphones / [edited by] Marsha
Berry, Royal Melbourne Institute of Technology, Australia ; Max
Schleser, Massey University, New Zealand.
pages cm
ISBN 978-1-137-48265-5 (hardback)
1. Video recordings—Production and direction. 2. Video
recordings—Social aspects. 3. Journalism—Technological innovations.
4. Smartphones. I. Berry, Marsha, editor. II. Schleser, Max, 1980– editor.

PN1992.94.M63 2014
384.55′8—dc23   2014030397

A catalogue record for this book is available from the British Library.

First edition: 2014

www.palgrave.com/pivot

DOI: 10.1057/9781137469816

Contents

List of Illustrations

Notes on Contributors

Crystal Abidin is a PhD candidate in Anthropology and Sociology at the University of Western Australia. She has been tracking the commercial blog industry in Singapore since August 2010. Crystal has published in journals including *Women's Studies International Forum*, *Limina*, and *Global Media Journal* (Australian Edition).

Craig Batty is creative practice research leader in the School of Media and Communication at RMIT University, Australia. He is author and co-author of five book and editor of the book *Screenwriters and Screenwriting: Putting Practice into Context* (2014). Craig is also a screenwriter, script editor, and script consultant with experiences on short film, feature film, television, and online projects.

Leo Berkeley is a senior lecturer in the School of Media and Communication at RMIT University in Melbourne, Australia. He also has considerable experience as an independent filmmaker, having written and directed the feature film. His current research interests are in the practice of screen production, low and micro-budget filmmaking, improvisation, essay films, community media, and machinima.

Marsha Berry is a senior lecturer and a digital ethnographer in the School of Media and Communication at RMIT University. Marsha is also an artist whose practice includes poetry, video art, and new media. She has explored notions of memory, place, and displacement through video art, photography, and poetry. As a

DOI: 10.1057/9781137469816.0003

part of this project, she runs a website that pins poetry to place http://poetry4u.org.

Edgar Gómez Cruz is a research fellow at the Institute for Communication Studies, University of Leeds. He has published widely on a number of topics relating to digital communications particularly in the area of digital photography, digital ethnography, and visual culture.

Fran Edmonds' research interests are interdisciplinary and include the intersection of Western and Indigenous knowledge systems, the reclaiming of Aboriginal material culture through digital technologies, and the exploration of collaborative methodological approaches to cross-cultural research. Fran's current research stems from her PhD, which focused on the continuation of southeast Australian Aboriginal art practices since colonisation.

Larissa Hjorth is an artist, digital ethnographer, and Professor in the Games Programs, School of Media & Communication, RMIT University. She is the co-director of RMIT's Digital Ethnography Research Centre (DERC) with Heather Horst. Since 2000, Hjorth has been researching the gendered and socio-cultural dimensions of mobile, social, locative, and gaming cultures in the Asia–Pacific.

Brian House is a media artist whose work traverses alternative geographies, experimental music, and a critical data practice. His work has been shown by MoMA (NYC), MOCA (LA), Ars Electronica, Cincinnati Contemporary Arts Center, and Eyebeam Art and Technology Center, among others, and has been featured in publications including *WIRED*, *TIME*, and *The New York Times*. He is currently a doctoral student at Brown University in the Music and the Modern Culture and Media departments.

Dean Keep is a lecturer/artist at Swinburne University, Melbourne. Dean has been actively researching mobile media, and producing mobile film and photography since 2004. Dean has exhibited mobile film and photography in both national and international forums. Dean's research has a strong focus on the ways that emergent media technologies inform creative practices. Dean is currently enrolled as a PhD candidate at the Canberra School of Art.

Patrick Kelly is an early career researcher and sessional teacher at RMIT's School of Media and Communication. As a freelance writer, he has had articles published on ABC's *The Drum*, *M/C Reviews* and in

DOI: 10.1057/9781137469816.0003

The Lifted Brow. His teaching and research investigates the experience of traditional and contemporary image-making forms and methods in the current technological age.

Adam Kossoff is an artist-filmmaker and writer, whose work addresses and questions the relationship of the moving image to different spatial and technological contexts. He is a reader in Moving Image at the University of Wolverhampton.

Cristina Miguel is a PhD candidate in Communications and a teaching assistant at the University of Leeds. She is also a part-time lecturer at Leeds Metropolitan University. Her PhD focuses on intimacy in the age of social media. She has recently worked as a research assistant on a project exploring social media monitoring and the social media industries.

Max Schleser is a filmmaker who explores mobile devices as creative and educational tools. His portfolio includes various experimental and collaborative documentary projects, which are screened at film and new media festivals internationally. Schleser co-founded the Mobile Innovation Network Aotearoa. He teaches video production and supervises MDes, MFA, and PhD students.

Eugenio Tisselli holds a degree in Computer Systems Engineering from Monterrey Institute of Technology and Higher Education in Mexico and a master's degree in Digital Arts from the UPF, and he is a member of the Hermeneia research group. He was co-director and lecturer on the UPF Masters course in Digital Arts. He is currently a PhD candidate at Z-Node: The Zurich Node of the Planetary Colegium. His research on mobile technologies and rural communities can be found at http://ojovoz.net

DOI: 10.1057/9781137469816.0003

1
Creative Mobile Media: The State of Play

Marsha Berry and Max Schleser

Abstract: *This chapter elaborates on the creative dimensions of mobile media practices point at prospects to further expand the field of creative arts and design. It contributes to existing debates around co-presence in networked media and the impact of smartphones on our understandings and interactions with space and place; emergent socialities associated with social media to contextualize the notion of 'sharing' and how this concept is replacing 'community'; the aesthetics of mobile media; and how storytelling shapes and is shaped by mobile media.*

Berry, Marsha and Max Schleser. *Mobile Media Making in an Age of Smartphones.* New York: Palgrave Macmillan, 2014. DOI: 10.1057/9781137469816.0004.

With the rise of smartphones in 2007 and the proliferation of applications (apps) through Apple's App Store and Android Market (now Google Play) in the following year, how citizen users and creative professionals represent, experience and share the everyday is changing. Gerard Goggin, a leading researcher in mobile media, proposed that there is a 'bewildering and proliferating array of cultural activities revolving around mobile phones' that shape how 'new ways of being of being oneself' (Goggin 2006, 2). The growing abundance of camera phone apps has allowed everyday users tools and techniques once available only to professionals. This ability to experiment with apps supports emergent visualities (Pink and Hjorth 2012), which are shaping how we take, share and contextualize images both still and moving. With the overlay of location-based services, these experiences and representations are providing new social, creative, and emotional cartographies, which in turn, have created new opportunities for creative practice over the past decade.

Writers, poets and visual artists, filmmakers, designers, finger-painters (as illustrators working with mobile devices call themselves) are using innovative forms within spaces created by social media where 'creative vernaculars' (Burgess 2008) and aesthetics are emerging. Mobile media remixes and remediates old and new media (Bolter and Grusin 1999) and also shapes storytelling to generate new forms. Numerous debates abound in mobile media around issues of telepresence and co-presence and how they are impacting on contemporary life. Rheingold saw the development of pervasive networked technology as a positive community building force claiming that computer-mediated communication had the potential to change the world. In 1993 he wrote that something 'big is afoot, and the final shape has not been determined' (n.p.). His theory of virtual communities shaped how many thought about computer-mediated communication and set a dominant paradigm. Recently other ways have emerged that seek to understand the complexity of social interactions and rituals that are facilitated by networked technology and smartphones. A departure from notions of community and networks as the dominant paradigms in thinking about mobile media (Postill and Pink 2012) can place the emphasis on sharing as a key aspect of the emergent socialities evident in mobile media and in turn, on how these shape and are shaped by creative practices.

The socialities and routine sharing practices evident in social media are underpinned by co-presence. The idea of presence and mediation

DOI: 10.1057/9781137469816.0004

in social interaction was theorized by Goffman in 1959 and can often be entangled with notions of authenticity where somehow face-to-face interactions are viewed as more authentic than online interactions. For example, Turkle (2011) advocates that we should spend less time using our smartphones because of potential adverse effects. Her argument is grounded in the notion that face-to-face encounters are richer and more demanding than online encounters. She looks back to the pre-smartphone age with nostalgia. On the other hand, Ito (2005) drew attention to the complexities of co-presence as important to sociality in her ethnographic studies of how Japanese youth used mobile phones to bring in physically absent friends into face-to-face social gatherings.

Co-presence (Goffman 1959; Ito 2005; Pink and Hjorth 2012) in the 21st century extends beyond face-to-face interactions into the realm of networked media and has an impact on our understandings and interactions with mundane places and spaces including public transport (Berry and Hamilton 2010). Smartphones have had a profound impact on our understandings and interactions with space and place. Emergent socialities associated with mobile social media are predicated on norms of reciprocity where images and status updates are shared and 'liked' on Facebook or retweeted on Twitter.

Mobile media making in the age of smartphones explores the creative practice that developed within the last 10 years. While there are a number of exhibitions, festivals, and screenings that showcase this emerging form of practice (Schleser 2011) only very few publications engage in the new field of study. The significance of mobile media has been the subject of several studies in cultural, audience, and media studies, including those of Rieser (2012), Goggin (2012), Farman (2011), Ling and Donner (2009), de Souza e Silva and Frith (2012), Katz, LaBar and Lynch (2011), and Snickars and Vonderau (2012). This book will attempt to define the recognition of a specific mobile form with an emphasis on mobile media making. Writing in *Mobile Media Research—State of the Art,* Goggin and Hjorth state point at the opportunities that mobile media provide for expression and agency (Goggin and Hjorth 2014, 1). These prospects of the proliferation of mobile filmmaking and photography, and the embedding of these creative practices in networked and social media illustrates developments that not only have an impact on smartphones but also the contemporary media ecology as a whole. Mobile media making introduces new practices, formats, and forms signifying avenues for creative innovation. This collection of essays emerges out of

DOI: 10.1057/9781137469816.0004

a symposium held on December 2013 in Melbourne, and addresses the theme of mobile media creativity in an age of smartphones.

The book reflects the scholarship of The Digital Ethnographic Research Centre (RMIT University) in partnership with the Mobile Innovation Network Aotearoa (MINA). The Digital Ethnography Research Centre (DERC) was established in 2012 as part of RMIT University's School of Media and Communication. Co-directed by Larissa Hjorth and Heather Horst, DERC seeks to foster cross-cultural, interdisciplinary, and multi-sited research around this important field in the Asia-Pacific region and beyond. Co-directed by Max Schleser (Nga Pae Māhutonga School of Design, Massey University, Wellington, NZ) and Laurent Antonzak (School of Art and Design, Colab and CfLAT, AUT University, Auckland) and established in 2011, MINA is an international network that seeks to promote cultural and research activities to expand the emerging possibilities of mobile media. MINA aims to explore the opportunities for interaction between people, content, and the creative industry within the context of Aotearoa/New Zealand and internationally. MINA have worked in collaboration with the iPhone Popup Film Festival (UK), the International Mobile Film Festival and iPhone Film Festival (USA), Mobile Film Festival (Macedonia), Mobilstreifen (Germany), New Zealand Film Archive (Wellingon, NZ), Ohrenblick Mal (Germany), Sesiff-Seoul International Extreme Short Image & Film Festival (Korea) to host screenings in New Zealand and Australia.

Scholars from across Australia, United Kingdom, United States of America. New Zealand, and France came together to discuss this exciting and significant phenomenon from research perspectives informed by creative practice and ethnography. This book brings together bring together several discipline areas—digital ethnography, filmmaking, photography, art, and media studies to provide new understandings of the emerging creative practices within the context of mobile media.

The chapters discuss the prospects of the proliferation of mobile and digital filmmaking opportunities—from citizen journalism to networked, transmedia collaborative filmmaking and photography in the realm of a social media landscape. This collection includes critical reflections on emergent creative practices as well as digital ethnographies of new visualities and socialities associated with smartphone cameras in every-day life. Framed through the lens of smartphone apps, this book reflects on the changing nature of media production and consumption and engages with contemporary debates concerning co-presence, aesthetics,

DOI: 10.1057/9781137469816.0004

co-presence in networked media, and the impact of smartphones on our understandings and interactions with space and place; emergent socialities associated with social media to contextualize the notion of 'sharing' and how this concept is replacing 'community'; the aesthetics of mobile media; and how storytelling shapes and is shaped by mobile media.

The book has been organized into four sections. Each of these sections addresses contemporary debates in mobile media and presents original research. We posed a broad research question to the authors: How do smartphone technologies help us rethink:

1. Aesthetics
2. Space and place
3. Knowledge and stories
4. The self

The chapters in the first section, *Aesthetics*, explore how smartphone cameras offer new creative possibilities to artists, photographers, and filmmakers. Keep's chapter opens this section. He commences the thread of exploring mobile media aesthetics in his chapter where he traces how the camera phone continues to remediate and refashion the tropes of traditional photography, thus giving rise to new image-making processes and new ways of seeing. He discusses the shape-shifting parameters of the camera phone and how these have impacted the field of photography through an examination of the ways in which camera phones have reconfigured our relationship with imaging and have facilitated new modes of photographic practice. He locates smartphone photography within broader discourses and theoretical frames of fine art photography.

Berkley's chapter is a reflective account focusing on creative practice. Berkley has a long career as a filmmaker and in this chapter he investigates the potential of the essay film to integrate creative and academic practices as a form of personal documentary about the experience of travelling on tram No. 57 in Melbourne. He addresses aesthetics in his reflection on the iPhone documentary Tram 57 by asking what are the aesthetic possibilities of smartphone cameras and what styles of films are enhanced given these possibilities? Kossoff interrogates how mobile films enhance the aesthetics of the spatiality of the moving image through a re-enactment of Benjamin's Moscow Diary. He used a camera phone for this film project and reflects upon his creative practice in this chapter.

The second section, *Space and Place*, explores the intersection of smartphone cameras with space and place. Hjorth discusses how

DOI: 10.1057/9781137469816.0004

location-based mobile games using camera phones can help to uncover psychological, playful, and emotional dimensions of place. She contextualizes her elucidation of two key concepts to creative mobile media—ambient play and intimate co-presence—through a discussion of an art project using smartphone cameras called keitai mizu (mobile water), which explored the intersections of public art, screen media, and climate change in Melbourne, Shanghai, and Tokyo. Berry focuses on photo sharing and emergent socialities and visualities. She proposes that the popularity of the faux-vintage filters common to Instagram as well as many other smartphone camera applications is more than simple nostalgia but rather symptomatic of a complex desire to share nuanced senses of place through mobile media. The final chapter in this section is by House who suggests that text messaging can serve as a narrative medium that subverts traditional boundaries in the experience of literature. He presents an original work, *The Wrench*, as an example of subversive mobile storytelling.

The third section, *Knowledge and Stories*, explores the nexus of mobile media, knowledge creation, and storytelling. Tisselli is one of the creators and coordinators of a collaborative knowledge base created by farmers in Tanzania. In this chapter he reports on how smartphones were used to document the work of the farmers and publish their observations about the effects of climate change through sharing images and voice recording online in order to expand their social networks. Edmonds reports on a digital storytelling project in which she is working with an Australian Aboriginal community to harness the creative potential of mobile digital devices for developing digital literacy and multimedia skills. She discusses how information is created and shared through social media and how the popularity of social media can be utilized to support Aboriginal youth culture and to reclaim Aboriginal material culture. The final chapter in this section, by Batty, takes the reader into the world of screenwriting and explores what happens when screenwriting becomes possible on a smartphone. He argues that smartphone apps provide a platform where screenwriters can be freed of the logistical side of writing a screenplay, which has enormous implications for screenwriting practices. Batty's chapter traces the impact of technology and its various functionalities and tools on the creative process of telling stories through screenplays. He rethinks what differences smartphones and apps bring to screenplay writing practices and knowledge construction in terms of storytelling models within the assemblages of

DOI: 10.1057/9781137469816.0004

mobile media as well as the evolving configuration between technology and the writer.

The fourth section, *The Self*, explore issues around self-expression and self-presentation in online worlds. Abidin uncovers a plethora of fascinating competitive strategies utilized by celebrity lifestyle bloggers who use their private lives as a tool in their quest to win attention and followers on the popular smartphone photo sharing application, Instagram. Kelly situates his exploration of self-expression as a film-maker through the discourses of Slow Media. He argues convincingly that apps such as Instagram can be used to create thoughtful and reflective media art that addresses the aesthetic concerns famously espoused by Walter Benjamin. In his chapter, Kelly suggests that films created with smartphone apps can evoke Benjamin's elusive aura. Gómez Cruz and Miguel present an ethnography that focuses on sexually mediated practices and how the normalization of these intimate mediations is being shaped through the lens of smartphone photography as a series of everyday practices.

They discuss how emplacement, co-presence, playfulness, and affordances construct creative ways to experience intimacy. Schleser examines the recent phenomenon of mobile filmmaking in the context of autobiographical film theory. He explores mobile devices as a tool for autobiographical filmmaking with a focus on a user-based interpretation of the autobiographical discourse.

Together, the chapters in this book provide a rich survey of social, mobile, personal, and creative practices and also address the defining character of mobile aesthetics. They make a valuable contribution to the growing field of mobile communication studies, while also focusing on the importance of creative dimensions, which are often overlooked in favor of social and cultural analysis. Overall, this collection presents innovative methods to better understand both the potential and challenges of creative practice framed by mobile media in an age of smartphones.

References

Berry, Marsha and Margaret Hamilton. 2010. 'Changing Urban Spaces: Mobile Phones on Trains', *Mobilities* 5(1): 111–31.

Bolter, Jay, D. and Richard Grusin. 1999. *Remediation: Understanding New Media*. Cambridge, MA: The MIT Press.

DOI: 10.1057/9781137469816.0004

Burgess, Jean. 2008. ' "All Your Chocolate Rain Are Belong to Us?": Viral Video, Youtube and the Dynamics of Participatory Culture', in G. Lovink and S. Niederer (eds), *The Video Vortex Reader*, Amsterdam: Institute of Network Cultures, 101–11.

De Souza e Silva, Adriana and Jordan Frith. 2012. *Mobile Interfaces in Public Spaces: Locational Privacy, Control, and Urban Sociability.* London: Taylor & Francis Group.

Farman, Jason. 2011. *Mobile Interface Theory: Embodied Space and Locative Media.* New York, NY: Routledge.

Goffman, Erving. 1959. *The Presentation of Self in Everyday Life.* New York: Doubleday.

Goggin, Gerard. 2006. *Cell Phone Culture: Mobile Technology in Everyday Life.* London: Routledge.

Goggin, Gerhard. 2012. *New Technologies and the Media (Key Concerns in Media Studies).* London: Palgrave Macmillan.

Goggin, Gerhard and Larissa Hjorth. 2014. *The Routledge Companion to Mobile Media.* London: Routledge.

Ito, Mizuko. 2005. 'Introduction: Personal, Portable, Pedestrian', in M. Ito, D. Okabe and M. Matsuda (eds), *Personal, Portable, Pedestrian: Mobile Phones in Japanese Life.* Cambridge, MA: MIT Press, 1–16.

Katz, James, E., Wayne, LaBar and Ellen Lynch. 2011. *Creativity and Technology: Social Media, Mobiles and Museums.* New York: MuseumsEtc.

Ling, Rich and Jonathan Donner. 2009. *Mobile Communication.* Cambridge, UK: Polity.

Pink, Sarah and Larissa Hjorth. 2012. 'Emplaced Cartographies: Reconceptualising Camera Phone Practices in an Age of Locative Media', *Media International Australia* 145: 145–56.

Postill, John and Sarah Pink. 2012. 'Social Media Ethnography: The Digital Researcher in a Messy Web' [online]. *Media International Australia* 145: 123–34.

Rheingold, Howard. 1993. *The Virtual Community.* Electronic version, retrieved from http://www.rheingold.com/vc/book/intro.html (accessed June 29, 2014).

Rieser, Martin. 2012. *The Mobile Audience: Media Art and Mobile Technologies.* Amsterdam: Rodopi.

Schleser, Max. 2011. *Mobile-mentary. Mobile Documentaries in the Contemporary Mediascape.* Sarbruecken: LAP Lambert Academic Publishing.

DOI: 10.1057/9781137469816.0004

Snickars, Pelle. and Patrick Vonderau. 2012. *Moving Data: The Iphone and the Future of Media*. New York: Columbia University Press.

Turkle, Sherry. 2011. *Alone Together: Why We Expect More from Technology and Less from Each Other*. New York: Basic Books.

DOI: 10.1057/9781137469816.0004

Part I
Aesthetics

Berry, Marsha and Max Schleser. *Mobile Media Making in an Age of Smartphones*. New York: Palgrave Macmillan, 2014. DOI: 10.1057/9781137469816.0005.

▶

DOI: 10.1057/9781137469816.0005

In the article *Aesthetics Mobile Media*, Baker, Schleser, and Molga (2009) attempt to define the at that time new category of Mobile Media Art. As one of the first publications dealing with the aesthetics of mobile media making, this pioneering effort explored the mobile video camera and mobile phones' connectivity to expand the domain of art and media practice. Despite the different approaches and backgrounds of the practitioners in moving image, performance, digital media, and visual art a shared original aesthetic specific to the mobile phone is discussed in terms of its personal, immediate, and intimate qualities. These characteristics are revealed in the discussed mobile-mentary (mobile documentary) (Schleser 2011) *Max With a Keita*, the mobile video and performance work *MindTouch* and the mobile visual art work *Little Heavens*.

Within a decade of mobile media making the tools developed from 3gp (176 × 144 pixels) to MPEG4 (1920 × 1080 pixels) video formats, Bluetooth to WiFi connectivity, MMS (multimedia messaging service) to live streaming and as Dean Keep points out from a 'plastic camera lens and the unsophisticated image sensor' to a 3.6 × f/1.8 Carl Zeiss zoom lens. In addition the proliferation of apps through Apple's app store and Andriod's market (now Google Play) since its launch in 2008 have expanded the possibilities for mobile media making. David Scott Leibowitz's *Mobile Digital Art* provides an example of 70 international artists using apps to make art and Taz Goldstein's *Hand Held Hollywood's Filmmaking with the iPad & iPhone* provides an overview of available apps for filmmaking (David 2013).

A detailed description of *Early Mobile Aesthetics as Intervention to the Industry dominated Discourse* (Schleser 2013) is provided in the MINA Special Issue in Ubiquity the Intellect Journal of Pervasive Media. Next to this Archaeology section referring to the work of Schleser, Kaganof, Barnard, Bliss, Reichhold, Hawley, Weberg, Massoni among other the Journal also features an interview with Columbian mobile filmmaker Felipe Cardona.

The above outlined qualities and key characteristics of personal media, presence, intimate, and immediate qualities are continuing to shape the current discourse of mobile media making. Baker, Schleser and Molga refer to Gye,

> Camera phones are not, however just another kind of camera. Located as they are in a device that is not only connected to the telecommunications grid but that is usually carried with us wherever we go, camera phones are both

DOI: 10.1057/9781137469816.0005

extending existing personal imaging practices and allowing for the evolution of new kinds of imaging practices. (Gye in Baker, Schleser, and Molga, 102)

Correspondingly, Keep argues over the past decade (2004–2014) the camera phone has played an important role in reconfiguring our relationship with photography, and has promoted a reimagining and remediation of the tropes associated with traditional cinema and photography. Writing in *Artist with a camera-phone: A decade of mobile photography* he expands the definition toward the formulation of a liquid aesthetic whereby ongoing developments in mobile and communication technologies are constantly shaping, then reshaping, the technical and creative parameters of the camera phone. He summarizes this through the 'Kodak moment' that has now been replaced by the 'mobile moment'. Leo Berkeley's chapter develops this notion into the realm of moving image-practice, drawing upon Campany (2007) 'these moments had the key additions of duration, movement and all the affective qualities associated with time and the moving image' and the context of the essay film. He argues that the smartphone is a device that incorporates a high-quality video camera can both be located within a long history of increasingly portable and accessible motion picture technology, as well as offering specific practical and aesthetic features that make it suitable for a personal, reflective style of documentary filmmaking such as that modeled by the essay film.

Adam Kossoff contextualizes his mobile-mentary (Schleser 2011) *Moscow Diary*, in which he revisits the streets and buildings Benjamin mentions, creating a visual locational map. By means of describing the phenomenological attributes of technics, temporal and spatial he outlines the influence of the mobile phone on our sense of time and space. The chapter *The mobile phone and the flow of things* also discusses the long take and its implications, which he used as a creative strategy in his work. Keep, Berkeley, and Kossoff's creative practice underline the notion of experience and presence that mobile media is establishing increasingly in relation with networked and social media.

The Aesthetics section in *Mobile Media Making* illustrates how creative practitioners further develop and refine independent, artistic, and avant-garde practices in the age of smartphones. These aesthetic developments pave the way for changes within the mediascape. The creative practice within this section and other mentioned examples throughout this book demonstrates the innovative capacity of mobile media.

DOI: 10.1057/9781137469816.0005

References

Baker Camille, Max Schleser and Kasia Molga. 2009. 'Aesthetics of Mobile Media Art' *Journal of Media Practice* 10 (2&3): 101–122.

Campany, David, ed. 2007. *The Cinematic*. London and Cambridge, MA: Whitechapel Gallery and The MIT Press.

David, Scott Leibowitz. 2013. *Mobile Digital Art*. Oxford: Focal Press.

Schleser, Max. 2011. *Mobile-Mentary. Mobile Documentaries in the Contemporary Mediascape*. Sarbruecken: LAP LAMBERT Academic Publishing.

Schleser, Max. 2013. 'Early Mobile Aesthetics as Intervention to the Industry Dominated Discourse'. *Ubiquity. The Journal of Pervasive Media*, 2 (1 & 2): 81–95.

Taz, Goldstein. 2012. *Hand Held Hollywood's Filmmaking with the iPad & iPhone*. San Francisco: Peachpit Press.

DOI: 10.1057/9781137469816.0005

2

Artist with a Camera-Phone: A Decade of Mobile Photography

Dean Keep

Abstract: *The camera-phone has emerged as the dominant device for the production and sharing of photographic images in the new millennium. No longer constrained by the technological parameters of the past, the camera-phone continues to remediate and refashion the tropes of traditional photography, thus giving rise to new image making processes and new ways of seeing. As camera-phone technology continues to evolve, these technological shifts have facilitated a liquid aesthetic that is constantly in flux. With this in mind, this research examines the shape-shifting parameters of the camera-phone and its impact on the field of photography; examining the ways in which camera-phones have reconfigured our relationship with imaging and facilitated new modes of photographic practice.*

Berry, Marsha and Max Schleser. *Mobile Media Making in an Age of Smartphones.* New York: Palgrave Macmillan, 2014. DOI: 10.1057/9781137469816.0006.

DOI: 10.1057/9781137469816.0006

The mobile phone, as suggested by Jenkins (2006, 5), is a central part of a convergence culture that is transforming our understanding of media and communication in the new millennium. In a 'database culture' (Manovich 2001) whereby digital assets may be understood as important forms of cultural and personal expression, mobile phones with cameras (camera phones) have emerged as powerful enablers for the capture, editing, storage, and sharing of digital images, thus promoting new ways to produce and experience photomedia.

Camera phone photography may be understood as a multi-faceted and dynamic imaging practice shaped by the constant ebb and flow of emergent communication technologies and the shape-shifting nature of mobile media. Over the past decade (2004–2014) the camera phone has played an important role in reconfiguring our relationship with photography, and has promoted a reimagining and remediation of the tropes associated with traditional cinema and photography.

For visual artists and/or photographers, the camera phone not only presents ways to extend one's photographic practice, but it also provides an opportunity to free creative practitioners from the theoretical and aesthetic conventions often associated with so-called 'professional' and/or 'fine art' forms of photography. Just as the release of Kodak's inexpensive and easy-to-use 'Brownie' camera in the 1890's transformed photography into an everyday leisure activity (Murray 2008, 152), the ubiquitous camera phone has transformed our relationship with photography in the digital age. The 'Kodak moment' has now been replaced by the 'mobile moment'.

Factors such as ease of use, connectivity, accessibility, and relative low-cost make the camera phone an ideal tool for capturing visual representations of personal and/or collective experiences, thus promoting a new understanding of the ways that photographs can be used to communicate and express ourselves within our everyday lives. Lee (2007, 24) suggests that camera phones not only 'reconstruct our experience of seeing' but they also challenge many of the established conventions associated with photography, such as social relations between the person/s being photographed and the photographer, as well as the worthiness and cultural meaning of popular photographs.

Digital photographs captured on camera phones are perhaps less bound by their referent, they are a type of 'hybrid media' that may be easily repurposed, remixed, and recontextualized for a wide variety of purposes and communications. From photographs of family, friends,

DOI: 10.1057/9781137469816.0006

and pets, through to travel snaps, food and self-portraits, the ubiquitous camera phone is often on hand to capture the evidence of our day-to-day lives. The camera phone not only presents us with new ways to capture photographic images, but it has also promoted a liquid aesthetic whereby ongoing developments in mobile and communication technologies are constantly shaping, then reshaping, the technical and creative parameters of the camera phone.

In this chapter, I suggest that camera phones remediate (Bolter and Grusin 2000) traditional photography; identifying factors that arguably contribute to the shape-shifting nature of camera phone technology, and in turn how these technological shifts have promoted a reimagining of photography and photographic practices in the mobile age. Drawing upon the fields of mobile media, photography and media archaeology, here I construct a loose cartography of the technological innovations and subsequent obsolescence that has informed camera phone photography over the past decade. In particular, I will refer to self-produced photographic and video work produced on camera phones (between 2004 and 2014) in Australia as a means of exploring and identifying the manner in which camera phones have influenced my own photographic practice.

Early camera phone photography

The camera phone is a transformative media tool that continues to shape our understanding of photography in the new millennium but as cellular networks and sophisticated smartphones with high-resolution cameras and editing software become more common-place, a review of camera phone photography and associated technological developments over the past decade may provide valuable insights for both artists and researchers. Developments in mobile media technology and cellular networks vary across the globe so, in order to better frame this research, I have situated my inquiry in relation to my own camera phone photographic practice in Australia between 2004 and 2014. From my first purchase of a camera phone in 2004 through to using a 5th generation iPhone operating on a 4G network in 2014, I have witnessed the rapid transformation of the camera phone from portable communication tool with imaging capabilities into a sophisticated portable media production and communications device.

DOI: 10.1057/9781137469816.0006

As an artist with a background in analog photography, I was keen to explore the perceived creative potential of the somewhat limited imaging capabilities of early model camera phones. Unlike the popular point-and-shoot digital single lens reflex (SLR) cameras of the time, early camera phone images were often prone to soft focus, de-saturated color and heavy pixilation. Defying the culture of 'sharp focus' so often associated with professional photography, early camera phone images often shared similarities with photographs produced by analog image making devices from the 1960s to 1970s, such as the Holga and Diana plastic film cameras, thus making the camera phone an ideal tool for remediating many of the tropes associated with experimental photography. Such technical shortfalls arguably led to a rejection of early model camera phones by professional photographers, and rather it was artists that were among the first to explore the potential of the camera phone for 'making art' and reimagining the photographic medium.

The plastic camera lens and the unsophisticated image sensor in early camera phone models made it difficult to achieve accurate renderings of subjects; perspectives were often stretched and colors were often muted or over-saturated. The tiny screen sizes of early model camera phones frequently made it difficult to frame subjects, especially in extreme light conditions; but perhaps in the hands of an artist, these so-called 'limitations' presented real opportunities to forge new creative frontiers whereby the perceived shortfalls of this emergent technology could be exploited for the production of innovative photographic practices.

Contemporary smartphone and social mobile media practices

Whereas traditional photography is arguably underpinned by a desire to document or preserve our memories of people, places, and events (see Barthes 1981; Benjamin 1936), it may be said that our growing acceptance of the camera phone in private and public spaces, along with our use of digital images on social media applications, has arguably played a role in the development of camera phone photographic genres. Unlike traditional photography, and its preoccupations with established aesthetic conventions; many of the subjects captured on camera phones are perhaps more associated with communicating aspects of personal

DOI: 10.1057/9781137469816.0006

experience with peers, rather than a preoccupation with 'correct' framing, lighting, and composition.

As observed by Hiorth (2007, 235) 'cameraphone practices are underscored by modes of realism. We feel like we are being allowed into someone's personal world—the ultimate fetishization of the personal'. Photographs of meals enjoyed, holidays, wine labels to be remembered for repeat purchase, haircuts to show off to friends, etc; indicate new ways of thinking about the way we use photography in our daily lives, rather than viewing photography as a static medium to be framed and hung on a wall. Camera phone photography is also less preoccupied with the production of a physical artifact (printed photographic image), rather it acknowledges the ways in which photographic images form a part of a complex visual language system that has evolved to fit the ever-changing parameters of our increasingly networked lives. The camera phone sits outside the field of traditional photography, therefore freeing users from the cultural baggage and conventions often associated fine art photographic practices. The size, portability and relative low-cost, makes the camera phone ideal for photographic experimentation.

In their paper 'The Social Life of Cameraphone Images', authors Van House and Davis (2007, 5) identify four areas that influence the production of camera phone images, citing 'creating and maintaining social relationships; constructing personal and group memory; self-presentation; and self-expression' as key drivers for the capturing and sharing of camera phone images. Photographic genres such as documentary, portraiture, and self-portraiture are potent signifiers of personal experience; they are a 'certificate of presence' (Barthes 1981, 87) that communicates to others the stories and relationships that form part of our lived experience. As suggested by Vitulano:

> Camera phone technology represents a serious shift in the role of photographic practices. Moving into the realm of being producers of identity through the exploration of the immediate, camera phones are subverting how owners are using and perceiving photography. (Vitulano 2011, 120)

The intimate nature of the camera phone makes it well placed as a device to aid the production and collection of autoethnographic artifacts in the form of photographs that reflect a myriad of personal narratives (Figure 2.1).

When recovering from a major illness, it seemed only right that I use this most intimate of media devices to capture photographic evidence of my two-year recovery period (2006–2007), after all it was the camera phone

DOI: 10.1057/9781137469816.0006

FIGURE 2.1   *Untitled 1 and Untitled 2, Recovery Series (2006)*

that had been there when I needed to communicate my thoughts and feelings with friends and family. Rather than isolating the photographs of my recovery period in a designated photo album the images remained stored on my phone, thus creating an entanglement of text messages, images, and memories. More than 300 self-portraits were captured on my camera phone, and by reviewing these images on a regular basis, I was able to use the camera phone as a portable visual diary to chart my progress throughout my recovery period.

Pixel practices

A lack of established photographic conventions for camera phones arguably promotes a culture of creative experimentation and presents new ways to view our world. A case in point is the image 'The Wait' (see Figure 2.2) which I produced for 'Order of Magnitude', an exhibition of camera phone photography held at the First Site gallery in Melbourne, 2007. Rather than be moan the poor image quality of early model camera phones, this series of digital images, produced by taking 72 dpi screen captures of mobile video played on a computer, set out to exploit the perceived technical limitations and celebrate the all too familiar 'soft aesthetic' of the camera phone.

The resulting camera phone images were then enlarged to highlight color shifts and produce excessive pixilation creating a visual effect reminiscent of the impressionist movement in painting. Images of highways and suburban streets, now take on an almost nostalgic quality. Pockets of soft focus and distortion, randomly generated by the camera phone, create

DOI: 10.1057/9781137469816.0006

FIGURE 2.2   *'The Wait' (2007) and 'Soft Rocket' (2007) from 'Order of Magnitude',* Dean Keep

areas of mystery within the frame, distorting the original image, disrupting the narrative, and creating a space for the viewer to project their own narrative interpretations. Just as the pinhole camera has taken its place as a transformative technology within the history of analog photography, it should be observed that these early models camera phones mark the beginning of an emergent mobile aesthetic located within the genealogy of digital imaging technologies and contemporary photographic practice.

iPhonography

The widespread introduction of Smartphone technology, and in particular the Apple iPhone, which went on sale in the U.S. June 2007, has been instrumental in ushering in a new wave of camera phone aesthetics and practices. Whereas earlier model camera phones had been constrained by limited technical capabilities, later model smartphones (with cameras) were designed to take advantage of the emerging location-based services and high-speed 3rd generation mobile communication networks. With greatly improved camera specifications (increased resolution and improved lens quality), touch screens and seamless integration of wireless communication networks, late model camera phones offer users unprecedented levels of media production tools and networking functionality.

The popularity of the iPhone, along with the photographic aesthetic it generates, has led to the development of a photographic genre called iPhonography. In her book 'The Art of iPhonography: A guide to Mobile

DOI: 10.1057/9781137469816.0006

Creativity', Roberts (2011, 7) defines iPhonography as 'the art of shooting and processing (editing and enhancing) digital images using an iphone'. According to the Apple website (www.apple.com.au) 'everyday more photos are taken with the iPhone than any other camera', so it would appear that the pocket-camera has now been replaced by the pocket camera phone. Hjorth (2007, 1) notes that:

> With almost all mobile phones now coming with cameras, many users—not necessarily interested in photography per se—are becoming avid practitioners in the making, circulating and socializing of their own images.

The iPhone, along with a host of dedicated photographic applications (apps), is the embodiment of a post-photoshop world whereby digital images may be remixed and re-contextualized to suit a host of moods and purposes. The integration of a high-resolution camera, editing software and photo filters, combined with the ability to easily upload images to social media sites, makes the iPhone, along with its Android counterparts, an ideal tool for participating in online social cultures where photographic images are frequently used as forms of both communication and 'cultural capital' (Bourdieu 1986).

According to Cruz and Meyer (2013, 216) the iPhone has instigated a 'fifth moment' in photography whereby photographic practices have become more fluid and photographers can sculpt or design their images on the same device as which they captured the image, thus establishing a more playful relationship with photography.

But it is not only smartphones with cameras that are shaping new photographic practices and aesthetics. Camera phone apps (Hipstamatic, Pixlr o matic and Mextures) that can be easily downloaded to the phone, as well as dedicated digital photography social media sites (http://pixlr.com, instagram.com), make it possible to readily change the appearance of photographic images (Figure 2.3).

FIGURE 2.3   *Examples of mobile app 'Pixlr o matic' filters applied to original camera phone image (far left) (2014), Dean Keep*

DOI: 10.1057/9781137469816.0006

Through the use of digital filters a single photograph can be altered in ways that invite new interpretations of photographic images, thus producing multiple translations of the original image. A black and white or sepia filter may be applied to imbue an image with a nostalgic quality, or scratches, dust and color casts suggestive of heritage media processes may be layered over images to create temporal shifts. Berry (2013) observes that:

The popularity of faux-vintage apps indicates that people are endeavoring to capture more than an accurate depiction of what their eyes can see. They are using heritage aesthetics to go beyond visual sense to interpret aspects of what the whole sensorium experiences as well as nostalgia for a strong sense of place. This desire to recreate the poetic dimensions of the auratic experiences we associate with analog media is evident in popular smartphone app filters (Berry, 2013, n.p).

The popularity of so-called 'retro apps' that mimic heritage media aesthetics has arguably generated a growing interest in film based photographic practices, perhaps best evidenced by the increased popularity of Holga film cameras and the recent return of the Polaroid film camera. This meshing of digital and analog photography promotes hybrid image making practices that help us to make connections between traditional and contemporary photographic processes and aesthetics.

Perhaps one of the most defining aspects of the new generation camera phones (smartphones) has been the introduction of GPS (Global Positioning Software) and location-based services. Hjorth and Pink (2014, 40) suggest that 'second-generation locative media and emerging contemporary camera phone practices are becoming entangled to create new visualities and socialities of place and place making'. Mobile applications such as Instagram, mesh locative media technologies, photo editing and image sharing capabilities, enabling users to seamlessly pin and share the location of images captured on camera phones, thus transforming the act of photography into both a creative and spatial practice.

Conclusion

Over the past decade, the camera phone has evolved from a portable communications device with basic image capture functions into a sophisticated media production tool capable of producing and disseminating high-definition digital images and video. In this ever shifting technological landscape, the camera phone continues to evolve, thus promoting a 'liquid aesthetic' whereby changes in technology, as well as our relationship with personal computing, may be understood as key drivers which shape image making practices.

Whereas once images captured on camera phones were perceived as existing outside of the sphere of professional and/or art photography, a growing number of dedicated camera phone photography competitions and exhibitions held around the world suggests that our understanding of photography has already shifted to include the camera phone. Events such as the Mobile Photography Awards at the Exposure gallery in Melbourne, Australia and the LA Mobile Art Festival run by iPhoneArt. com (IPA) in Santa Monica, U.S., which require participants to print their camera phone images for display on a gallery wall, play an important role in locating camera phone photography within an arts context, thus further legitimizing the use of camera phones for the production of photographic images in both amateur and professional creative spheres.

Camera phones have emerged as ideal tools for capturing and sharing the visual traces of the everyday via social media, but camera phones, and in particular smartphones *have arguably ushered in a 'new way of seeing'* that exploits the creative potential of mobile media devices and associated software *to create* a new visual grammar that arguably extends our understanding of photography and the role of the photographic image in our lives.

References

Barthes, Roland. 1981. *Camera Lucida*. New York: Hill and Wang.

Benjamin, Walter. 1936. 'The Work of Art in the Mechanical Age of Reproduction', retrieved from http://www.marxists.org/reference/subject/philosophy/works/ge/benjamin.htm (Accessed June 23, 2014).

Berry, Marsha. 2013. 'Haunted Smartphone Moments: Filtering a Sense of Place'. Paper presented at the Mina 3rd Mobile Mobile Creativity and Innovation Symposium, Auckland, New Zealand, November 21–22.

Bolter, Jay, and Richard Grusin. 2000. *Remediation: Understanding New Media*. Cambridge: MIT Press.

Bourdieu, Pierre. 1986. 'The forms of capital'. In John Richardson (ed.), *Handbook of Theory and Research in the Sociology of Education*. Westport, CT: Greenwood, 241–258.

DOI: 10.1057/9781137469816.0006

Cruz, E. G. and Eric. T. Meyer. 2012. 'Creation and Control in the Photographic Process: iPhones and the emerging fifth moment of photography.' *Photographies* 5 (2): 203–221. Accessed March 2, 2014. doi: 10.1080/17540763.2012.702123.

Hjorth, Larissa. 2007. 'Snapshots of Almost Contact: the Rise of Camera Phone Practices and a Case Study in Seoul, Korea.' *Continuum: Journal of Media & Cultural Studies* 21: 227–238.

Hjorth, Larissa and Sarah Pink. 2014. 'New Visualities and the Digital Wayfarer: Reconceptualizing Camera Phone Photography and Locative Media.' *Mobile Media & Communication* 2: 40–57. doi: 10.1177/2050157913505257.

Jenkins, Henry. 2006. *Convergence Culture: Where Old me and New Media Collide.* New York: New York Press.

Lee, Dong Hoo. 2007. 'How Cameraphones Reconstruct Our Experience of Seeing.' In Larissa Hjorth (ed.), *Waiting for Immediacy.* South Korea: IDP Printers/ Yonsei University, 24.

Manovich, Lev. 2001. *The Language of New Media.* Cambridge: MIT Press.

Murray, Susan. 2008. 'Digital Images, Photo-Sharing, and Our Shifting Notions of Everyday Aesthetics', *Journal of Visual Culture* 7: 147. Accessed March 3, 2014. doi: 10.1177/1470412908091935.

Roberts, Stephanie C. 2011. *The Art of iPhonography: A Guide to Mobile Creativity.* United Kingdom: The Ilex Press Limited.

Van House, Nancy A. and Marc Davis. 2005. 'The Social Life of Cameraphone Images.' Paper presented in *Workshop on Pervasive Image Capture and Sharing: New Social Practices and Implications for Technology Workshop (PICS 2005) at the Seventh International Conference on Ubiquitous Computing (UbiComp 2005) in Tokyo, Japan, 2005.*

Vitulano, Robert. 2011. 'Creating Cellular Vision: Cell Phone Photography and the (Shifting) Photographic Eye.' *McMaster Journal of Communication* 8: 117–134.

DOI: 10.1057/9781137469816.0006

3

Tram Travels: Smartphone Video Production and the Essay Film

Leo Berkeley

Abstract: *The use of the smartphone as a high-quality video camera has opened up a range of new creative possibilities for documentary filmmaking, taking advantage of these mobile devices' extreme portability to move closer to Astruc's dream of the camera-stylo, 'a means of writing just as flexible and subtle as written language'. This chapter looks at the production of a short essay film called 'the 57', about a tram route in Melbourne, using it as a case study to explore the opportunities for mobile phones to support new forms of filmmaking about the experience of everyday life. 'The 57' was shot entirely with an iPhone. The chapter reflects on considering the aesthetic possibilities associated with smartphones and the ways they can support a sustainable approach to micro-budget filmmaking in an academic research context.*

Berry, Marsha and Max Schleser. *Mobile Media Making in an Age of Smartphones.* New York: Palgrave Macmillan, 2014. DOI: 10.1057/9781137469816.0007.

This chapter examines the production of an essay film called the 57 (Berkeley 2013a) that was shot entirely with a smartphone (Apple iPhone 4S). The film builds on a previous body of work by the filmmaker, mainly in narrative drama and in the low and no-budget sector, which explores aspects of life that are often neglected in mainstream cinema, such as the world of work and daily routine, what could be described as the ordinary rather than the extraordinary. The 57 takes this focus and applies it to the essay film, as a form that allows an interest in everyday life to be explored from a different perspective, incorporating diverse elements of video and audio material into a personal, reflective documentary style that seeks to capture a sense of lived human experience.

While the essay film is a varied and hybrid filmic form, with many arguing it is defined by its liminal qualities (Arthur 2003, 59; Corrigan 2011, 8; Renov 2004, 72), it has long been associated with notions of the everyday. Key exponents of the essay film have used it to explore the nature of their personal and everyday experience in a broader social, political, and historical context. *Sherman's March* (McElwee 1986), while on one level retracing the route of a military campaign by a Civil War general, is far more concerned with conveying an intimate, auto-biographical self-portrait of a man searching for love. Agnes Varda's celebrated essay film *The Gleaners and I* (2000) deals with ageing and the passage of time, food waste, and a concern 'with the everyday minutiae typically excluded from fiction' (Wilson 2002, 1).

These films took advantage of production tools that, at the time, were considered small, lightweight, and liberating to use, while still allowing a level of picture and sound quality that would make them accessible to film and television audiences. *Sherman's March* was shot on 16mm film and, in an interview with the filmmaker, he has variously discussed the camera he used for shooting the film as a weapon, a device to pick up women, and an object to hide behind. However, his use of this camera also reflects the desire of many essay filmmakers to document their everyday life:

> I was almost always ready to shoot. I kept the camera within reaching distance, sometimes balanced on my shoulder. (MacDonald and McElwee 1988, 20)

By 2000, Agnes Varda made *The Gleaners and I* on DV video, celebrating the freedom it offered (Anderson and Varda 2001) and the 'first-person, artisan film-making' it allowed (Darke 2001, 32).

DOI: 10.1057/9781137469816.0007

It will be argued in this chapter that the evolution of the smartphone into a device that incorporates a high-quality video camera can both be located within a long history of increasingly portable and accessible motion picture technology, as well as offering specific practical and aesthetic features that make it suitable for a personal, reflective style of documentary filmmaking such as that modeled by the essay film.

The Film—*the 57*

The 57 is about a tram route that goes into and out of the city of Melbourne, Australia. The initial motivation for choosing this subject matter was to capture and reflect upon the dramatic incidents that frequently occurred, where drunk, unruly and other variously troubled passengers would transgress the unwritten boundaries of public transport behavior normally observed. Conveying the experience of being on the 57 tram in its various sensory and social dimensions was another objective—the things seen, thought, felt, and the way people relate or do not relate to those around them. Features of the broader public transport experience that ethnographic and sociological studies have captured through words, *the 57* attempted to convey through the creative use of a smartphone camera (Auge 2002, 8 and 50; Moran 2005, 51).

The aesthetic possibilities of mobile cameras

The broader questions considered during the production process for *the 57* film were: what are the aesthetic possibilities of smartphone cameras? And, what styles of film are enhanced given these possibilities?

In 2009, Baker, Schleser, and Molga highlighted the experimental status of mobile media documentary based on a pixelated, low-resolution aesthetic in an HD world, saying 'the mobile media device is a new medium for expression and experience, with its own unique aesthetics' (Baker et al. 2009, 119). In the few years since, smartphones have joined the HD world and the transition in image quality from low to high resolution has also shifted the blurred boundary in mobile movies between professional and nonprofessional practices (Cunningham 2012, 3; Schleser 2014, 157). It is in this in-between space that a film like *the 57* is positioned, taking advantage of the confluence of accessible

DOI: 10.1057/9781137469816.0007

high-quality image capture devices and new methods of distribution to explore opportunities for filmmakers operating outside mainstream forms and approaches. Schleser has argued that the emerging aesthetic specific to mobile movies, which he describes with the term 'Keitai aesthetic', highlights 'the experience of location and notions of personal, immediate, and intimate qualities' (Schleser 2014, 163). These qualities can be seen in recent mobile movies, such as *Two Stories* (Omareen 2013), which integrates a dramatic autobiographical reflection with prosaic and location-specific images, *North* (Kelly 2013), one of many recent mobile movies that deals with questions of the personal and place, or *Commute* (Willis 2013), which like *the 57* deals with the public transport experience but in a more purely visual way. All these productions convey how 'the notion of the everyday underlines the personal character of the mobile moving-image works' (Schleser 2014, 160).

Hyper-accessibility

The production of *the 57* highlighted how the principal advantage of using a mobile camera is its extreme portability. For example, *the 57* was shot over an extended period of time, intermittently and when the opportunity arose. On one occasion, while driving home it appeared that police cars were surrounding a 57 tram. It was straightforward in this situation to get out and take shots of what was happening in an immediate and unpremeditated way. Perhaps more importantly, with a smartphone it was also possible to capture the routine repetition of a daily activity, including in the film multiple shots of a trip on the tram, which reflected both the similarities and differences in the experience across time. The routine aspects of the experience were central to what was being expressed in the film, which was to convey important qualities of everyday experience. Logistically this would have been much more difficult to achieve with a bigger camera and arguably the more intrusive equipment would have produced a different creative outcome as well.

The history of portable camera technology

It is worth stressing that this hyper-accessibility is not a radical break with existing screen production practice, but rather a significant development

DOI: 10.1057/9781137469816.0007

with strong historical precedents. There are continuities with the history of increasingly portable screen production technology and the aesthetic movements aligned to it since at least the mid-20th century.

Tweedie (2013) has recently made similar connections in relation to DV production, linking it to the Italian neorealism movement shortly after World War 2, and the French New Wave in the late 1950s and 1960s 'when a new generation of portable cameras facilitated a low-budget, relatively unfettered mode of production' (cxii). Neupert (2007, 40) has also highlighted the role of newly available lightweight camera technology in relation to the French New Wave and similar points have been made by King (2005, 108) in relation to American Independent Cinema and Rascaroli (2012) with reference to the emergence of video in the 1980s as an alternative to film for the purposes of personal filmmaking:

> it is certainly true that video, thanks to its inexpensiveness, immediacy, wide availability and versatility, facilitates experimentation more easily than the cinema. (59)

The link between the accessibility of production technology and the potential for increased experimentation is one that has informed screen production history and can be seen in the emergence and increasing use of smartphone cameras. How this potential can be realized was a question the production of *the 57* was designed to explore, specifically in relation to new possibilities for a personal, reflective style of filmmaking. Pursuing this line of inquiry led to a focus on the essay film as a creative form.

Writing with a cameraphone

Alexandre Astruc is a key contributor to this issue with his influential 1948 essay La Camera-Stylo (Astruc 2009), where he said:

> the cinema will gradually break free from the tyranny of what is visual, from the image for its own sake, from the immediate and concrete demands of the narrative, to become a means of writing just as flexible and subtle as written language. (32)

Interestingly, in this article Astruc explicitly linked traditional cinema to its dominant means of exhibition at that time (i.e. screening in an auditorium) and suggested that moving away from this physical space

DOI: 10.1057/9781137469816.0007

would free up new possibilities for the aesthetics of cinema (ibid., 33). He also identified the potential for accessible motion picture camera technology to allow films to be made in different ways, suggesting something like the essay film might be one of those ways.

Corrigan argues that what essay films have in common are three qualities: personal expression, public experience, and the process of thinking (2011, 14). More specifically, as an essay film, *the 57* was designed, as Corrigan puts it, to explore 'interior and exterior geographies of everyday life' (106). Based on the experience of *the 57* production, using a smartphone camera enable this to be achieved in creatively interesting ways. As the voice-over in the film attempted to convey, much of the public transport experience is about the proximity of bodies, the invasions of personal space, the constant physical movement and the peculiar quality of privacy in a public space that combines to create a flow of everyday experience, a flow that arguably can be expressed with more complexity and nuance through moving images than words and is able to be captured particularly well through the use of a smartphone camera.

Physically and socially integrated into the environment being filmed, the act of recording video images in this situation felt very close to the concept of taking a 'snap' that is commonly associated with amateur still photography. If something of interest was seen, there was little or no impediment to taking the phone out and filming it, the practical barrier between thought and action accelerating the creative objective Varda highlighted with her move to DV video from film: 'to collapse the time lapse between wanting to film something and actually being able to do it' (Darke 2001, 32). The aesthetic implications of this were, like the process of taking 'snaps', the collection of images that reflected fragmentary moments of seen experience. However, unlike still photography, these moments had the key additions of duration, movement and all the affective qualities associated with time and the moving image (Campany 2007).

The shooting process through which this occurred was not so much a structured and coherent screen production experience as something more impressionistic, opportunistic, and fragmented. The focus of the filming with this camera was on moments of experience, often brief and transient moments, like the look out the tram window at something that captures one's attention but then is gone from sight. This quality of the ephemeral intersection of movement and time that motion pictures can capture is something a film essayist like Chris Marker has highlighted, what he referred to as 'the fragility of those moments suspended in time'

DOI: 10.1057/9781137469816.0007

in the voice-over to *Sunless* (1983, 2:23) and with significant shots and sequences in films like *Sunless* and *La Jetée* (1962) explicitly addressing it. See the celebrated image in *La Jetée* (1962, 19:50), a film otherwise composed entirely of still images, where the close-up of a woman subtly and briefly has movement, or the section in *Sunless* involving attempts to film the women in a market in Guinea-Bissau and the glance by one of them directly at the camera, 'the real glance that lasts 1/24 of a second, the length of a film frame' (*Sunless* voice-over 1983, 34:28).

An aesthetic interest in the creative depiction of these 'moments of experience' can also be found in the field of improvised drama and has even been argued as central to the film viewing experience itself:

> The moment, inevitably, is what we remember and retain, what we possess of the screen and incorporate into ourselves and our worlds. (Pomerance 2008, 6)

Of course, like the production of an improvised drama, the challenge with *the 57* was how to structure the mass of fragmented material collected in a way that conveyed the complexities of the lived experience while still being sufficiently coherent to interest the proposed audience.

Conclusion

In exploring the aesthetics of mobile movies through the production of the film *the 57*, the extreme portability of the camera, the collapsing of the time when filming between thought and action and the ability of the filmmaker to immerse themselves in a specific location and time were identified as the key features of the experience. While these features can be located within a long history of increasingly accessible motion picture technology, the smartphone camera has taken them to a new level. Supporting Schleser's work on the Keitai aesthetic (2014), the aesthetic qualities that emerged as a result involved the ability to convey on screen immediate but fragmented moments of lived experience relating to routine and everyday social activities from a distinctively personal perspective.

The theme of mobility became increasingly prominent while making this film, as it applied to both the subject matter and the means of production. Films shot with a smartphone camera are sometimes called mobile movies but it is clear there are different forms of mobility. The

DOI: 10.1057/9781137469816.0007

experience of regularly travelling on the 57 tram highlighted how a tram trip is about movement on rails. In the same way, the experience of making a mobile movie highlighted not only the freedoms it offered but also the constraints it imposed, some of which were more immediately apparent than others.

The hyper-accessibility of the camera was able to create the feeling that it was possible to film anything at any time but, during the production of *the 57*, this was not the case. There was an unwillingness, for example, to take shots of the rowdy men who were almost always down the back of the tram. These inhibitions were influenced by a wish not to be intrusive, sometimes a wish not to be physically assaulted but also by a sense that filming these incidents would distort them and not capture the experience effectively. The consequence was a production lacking the dramatic images that filmmakers commonly desire in a documentary.

On reflection, however, it could be said that what resulted was a production that captured the complexities of the process more authentically than initially thought. The inability to intrude on people to film them is like the reluctance to interact many passengers feel on public transport in other respects. This aspect of the experience is much commented on in the literature on commuting. Moran (2005) identifies 'the minimal acknowledgement of fellow passengers' as the definitive experience on the Paris Metro and the London Tube (54). In the end, perhaps unintentionally, the partial, impressionistic, and fragmented picture of the experience imposed by practicalities and these ethical and behavioral concerns, to some extent reflected the unmediated nature of the experience better than if it had been planned it that way.

References

Anderson, Melissa and Agnes Varda. 2001. "The Modest Gesture of the Filmmaker—an Interview with Agnes Varda', *Cineaste* 26 (4): 24–27.

Arthur, Paul. 2003. 'Essay questions from Alain Resnais to Michael Moore: Paul Arthur gives a Crash Course in Nonfiction Cinema's most Rapidly Evolving Genre', *Film Comment* 39 (1): 58–62.

Astruc, Alexandre. 2009. 'The Birth of the New Avant-Garde: Le Camera-Stylo.' In Peter Graham and Ginette Vincendeau (eds), *The French New Wave: Critical Landmarks*. London: Palgrave Macmillan on behalf of the British Film Institute, 31–38.

DOI: 10.1057/9781137469816.0007

Auge, Marc. 2002. *In The Metro*. Minneapolis: University of Minnesota Press.

Baker, Camille, Max Schleser, and Kasia Molga. 2009. 'Aesthetics of Mobile Media Art.' *Journal of Media Practice* 10 (2&3): 101–122.

Campany, David, ed. 2007. *The Cinematic*. London and Cambridge, MA: Whitechapel Gallery and The MIT Press.

Commute. 2013. Directed by Grant Willis. Australia: ZWI Films. https://vimeo.com/71701298. Motion Picture.

Corrigan, Timothy. 2011. *The Essay Film: From Montaigne, after Marker*. New York: Oxford University Press.

Cunningham, Stuart. 2012. 'Emergent Innovation through the Coevolution of Informal and Formal Media Economies', *Television & New Media* 13 (5): 415–430.

Darke, Chris. 2001. 'Refuseniks (Agnes Varda's DV Documentary, the "Gleaners and I")', *Sight and Sound* 11 (1): 30–33.

The Gleaners and I. 2000. Directed by Agnes Varda. France: Cine Tamaris. Motion Picture.

King, Geoff. 2005. *American Independent Cinema*. London: I.B. Tauris & Co. Ltd.

La Jetée. 1962. Directed by Chris Marker. France: Argos Films. Motion Picture.

MacDonald, Scott and Ross McElwee. 1988. 'Southern Exposure: An Interview with Ross McElwee', *Film Quarterly* 41 (4): 13–23.

Moran, Joe. 2005. *Reading the Everyday*. New York: Routledge.

Neupert, Richard. 2007. *A History of the French New Wave Cinema*. Madison, Wisconsin: University of Wisconsin Press.

North. 2013. Directed by Patrick Kelly. Australia: Patrick Kelly. MINA 3rd International Mobile Innovation Screening. DVD.

Pomerance, Murray. 2008. *The Horse Who Drank The Sky: Film Experience Beyond Narrative and Theory*. New Brunswick, New Jersey: Rutgers University Press.

Rascaroli, Laura. 2012. 'The Self-Portrait Film: Michelangelo's Last Gaze', In Alisa Lebow (ed.), *The Cinema of Me: The Self and Subjectivity in First Person Documentary*. London and New York: Wallflower Press, 57–78.

Renov, Michael. 2004. *The Subject of Documentary*. Minneapolis: University of Minnesota Press.

Schleser, Max. 2014. 'A Decade of Mobile Moving-Image Practice', In Gerard Goggin and Larissa Hjorth (eds), *Routledge Companion to Mobile Media*. New York: Routledge, 157–170.

DOI: 10.1057/9781137469816.0007

Sherman's March. 1986. Directed by Ross McElwee. USA: Ross McElwee. Motion Picture.

Sunless (Sans Soleil). 1983. Directed by Chris Marker. France: Argos Films. Motion Picture.

The 57. 2013a. Directed by Leo Berkeley. Australia: Leo Berkeley. https://vimeo.com/72173818. Motion Picture.

The 57 (MINA mix). 2013b. Directed by Leo Berkeley. Australia: Leo Berkeley. https://vimeo.com/75683029. Motion Picture.

Tweedie, James. 2013. *The Age of New Waves: Art Cinema and the Staging of Globalization*. Oxford: Oxford University Press.

Two Stories. 2013. Directed by Zaher Omareen. UK: Zaher Omareen. MINA 3rd International Mobile Innovation Screening. DVD.

Wilson, Jake. 2002. 'Trash and Treasure: The Gleaners and I', *Senses of Cinema* 23 (December): http://sensesofcinema.com/2002/feature-articles/gleaners/.

DOI: 10.1057/9781137469816.0007

4

The Mobile Phone and the Flow of Things

Adam Kossoff

Abstract: *This chapter investigates how the mobile phone film rewrites the way in which time and space are represented by the moving image. Bernard Stiegler's ideas around technics are central to the analysis. The experimental documentary film, Moscow Diary (2010) will form the basis for exploration of the technical and aesthetic production of the moving image. Walter Benjamin, the German essayist and cultural commentator, wrote Moscow Diary in 1926–1927. Based on the diary, the film is an urban journey through Moscow, contrasting two very different historical periods. Made on a mobile phone, it explores the social and political changes between Benjamin's view of 1920's Moscow and contemporary Moscow. The film focuses attention on the production of the image itself as well as the way in which mobile phone films enhance the spatiality of the moving image.*

Berry, Marsha and Max Schleser. *Mobile Media Making in an Age of Smartphones.* New York: Palgrave Macmillan, 2014. DOI: 10.1057/9781137469816.0008.

Nothing dates a cinema film more than a character with a cell phone that belongs to the recent past. In For New Critique of the Economy, Stiegler writes that, 'It is within this epoch of mafia capitalism...that one sees develop the systematic state lie, drive-based politics, and an addictive consumerism induced by industrial populism' (Stiegler 2010, 63). The fictionalized Gordon Gecko, there when 'mafia capitalism' went into overdrive, famously appears in the 1987 film *Wall Street* with a phone nicknamed the *Brick*, for obvious reasons. Given the *Bricks* huge price tag, around £7,000 in today's money, it is not surprising that only the 'greed is good' guru of corporate raiding could afford it. So there is a sign of things to come: bankers, corruption and global financialization, and the mobile phone, one large brick in the wall of neo-liberal economics. Gordon Gecko's phone soon became a must have consumer item, and as with the introduction of the car, time and space contracted amidst the increasing flow of everyday life.

Giorgio Agamben, following Martin Heidegger writes: 'For this reason the man who becomes bored finds himself in the "closest proximity"... to animal captivation' (2004, 64). Note the proximity of Gecko's animal nature and his relationship to the mobile phone. This theme of the animal/human, or the organic versus the inorganic, requires a some- what speculative investigation through the prism of *originary technicity*. This centers on the claim that all human evolution and activity has been formed by its relationship to the technological. Humankind, it is argued, has evolved in and through its relationship to technology. The 'technological turn' that has taken place in contemporary thinking will form the basis of my approach in the first part of this chapter. Following this, I will focus on the mobile phone as a video-making tool with its own political and aesthetic qualities, both in terms of my own filmmak- ing practice, the filmmaker as flâneur, and in terms of global resistance movements.

The epochal moment for the mobile phone came when it was made readily available as an object of mass consumption during the 1990s. Text messaging was first introduced in 1993 then the first smartphone and the first camera phone came along in 2002, followed by the Apple iPhone, with a touch screen, in 2007. The machine became a direct extension to the body, twenty-four seven. The contemporary smartphone is also an object of desire, that can track our every movement that allows the every- day to move that bit faster with more connectivity that has a 'corporate soul' at its centre, but also one that can be used as an ally in the resistance

DOI: 10.1057/9781137469816.0008

against oppression and authority. Consequently, the disconnected and fragmented world of the distant but engaged flâneur was replaced by a miniature machine at the end of an arm that engendered an absorption that contracted space and time, made all communication immediate and cut away the boredom of the everyday. Further on, I will discuss further the notion of the 'flâneur with a smartphone' in the context of my film *Moscow Diary* (2011), based upon Walter Benjamin's Moscow Diary and filmed on a smartphone.

The epochal

Originary technicity, a philosophy of technology, forwards the view that the human cannot be seen autonomously outside of its relationship to technology. Human life is distinguished by, and dependent upon the technological. Derived from the Greek, *techné*, technics states the machine 'as the instrument of man's production of himself and the world' (Bradley 2011, 22). Epochal evolutionary in changes in human life are often defined by technological change, Neolithic to bronze age or analog to digital age. Human evolution is predicated upon and integrated with the technology we use, whether it's the carved flint tools of Neolithic times, or the car from more recent times. Like the car, the introduction of the cell phone, arguably represents an epochal change in the way we live and behave.

Present-to-hand

Bradley argues that from the beginning of western metaphysics, 'technology is thus consigned into the darkness of the unthought' (2011, 3). Karl Marx is regarded as the first to take a position against the idea that the technical is a supplement waiting to be used, where the organic human oversees an inorganic world of its own invention. Instead, Marx argued that man is a tool-making animal, with the net result that the dialectical relationship between labor and the machine is the driver of historical materialism. Similarly, Friedrich Engels's speculative argument on the dialectical relationship between man and tools is well known; the human came into being through standing upright and using their upper limbs to create new skills.

DOI: 10.1057/9781137469816.0008

For Martin Heidegger *techné*, or technics, is central to the issue of our being, *Dasein*. Nature, Aristotle's *phusis*, exists as a reserve, a resource, for what is to be disclosed, formed and made; an embryonic process that gains its poetic *beingness* by calling upon that which awaits its labor as an immanent coming-into-being. The hammer serves as Heidegger's example of the *ready-to-hand*, when the human and technics is at one, each serving the other in a unity, bringing nature's reserve into our existence as part of our *beingness*. If the hammer breaks then this unity, and our reflection in our work, is disrupted. The tool then becomes *present-to-hand*, and the spell of immanent oneness is broken.

How far the mobile phone can take on this role of the hammer is up for question. No doubt it serves as an extension of the body, no doubt it aspires to the absorbed world of the *ready-to-hand*, and no doubt it is also present-to-hand to those who aren't familiar with it, or when it breaks down. Nevertheless, this state of absorption is an ideal that the mobile phone cleverly aspires toward. This is one reason why the cheap labor that makes the phone, and the exploitation of the scarce minerals that are so crucial to its working, can so easily be forgotten. Or, taking our cue from Heidegger, the exploitation of natural resources to make the mobile phone represents an enframing or *das Gestell*, the dangerous exploitation of nature for our own ends, rather than for what nature has to offer us. It is for this reason that we can say the mobile phone, despite its mnemonic qualities, after all we can consult it at the slightest memory lapse, suffers from selective memory through its fetishistic form.

Time and space

Through his ongoing analysis of originary technics, Bernard Stiegler challenges the view that the human is organic, over and above the technical. Following Heidegger and Jacques Derrida, Stiegler has consistently argued for the centrality of technics. The technological, the mnemotechnical in particular, embodies a temporality that is central to our experience and understanding of the world we live in. Edmund Husserl's phenomenological understanding of time falls short for Stiegler who argues that we need not only experience time in the present and then as it moves from the present into the past, as with the obvious example of music. But for Stiegler since we experience music,

DOI: 10.1057/9781137469816.0008

films, television and so on, via the technical, there will be always be a tertiary part to our understanding of time, that which is mediated by technology. So memory resides within technology, whether it is a clay pot or a Hollywood film. As human consciousness is formed through the temporal organization of the primary, present into the secondary past, via the tertiary of mnemotechnology, Stiegler has outlined how Hollywood films exploit the industrialization of time and so undermine the individuality of the spectator. Hollywood cinema, Stiegler argues, packages and compresses time, undermining its audiences the potentiality of individuation.

There has to my mind, been too much on time in Stiegler's thinking and in the general dissemination of his work. He does though discuss the way in which the Neolithic Bedolina Rock, a map carved into the rock above a plane, allows spatial awareness to come into existence: 'This exceptional place shows how the map makes orientation possible: as a process of reduction, selection and symbolization, in which *the space on the map contracts the territorial space in the same way as we see life-time contracted by cinema-time*' (Stiegler 2003). Furthermore, this mnemotechnological map, has sustained a spatial orientation for the generations that have followed. These phenomenological attributes of technics, temporal and spatial, form the best axes with which to think about the influence of the mobile phone on our sense of time and space.

The flâneur

One wonders whether the mobile phone facilitates the contemporary flâneur? That is the urban wanderer who individualizes time and space by remaining outside of the metropolitan crowds and the cut and thrust of the city. Walter Benjamin was the arch exponent of the unexpected encounter, the flâneur who investigated the origins of modernity and its roots in the past, together with the effects of industrialization on contemporary urban life's labyrinthine and ever-shifting experiences.

My film, *Moscow Diary* (2011), was filmed on a mobile phone and retraces Benjamin's steps by following the diary he wrote during his visit toward the end of 1926, until he left in the middle of January 1927. Benjamin's thinking on the epochal changes caused by the introduction of cinema, where he brought together the aesthetic of the diminished

DOI: 10.1057/9781137469816.0008

aura and the phenomenological changes in perception and his writing on the urban and the flâneur, inspired my use of the mobile phone. Revisiting the streets and buildings Benjamin mentions, *Moscow Diary* creates a visual locational map. Using contemporary images of Moscow whilst relating the edited diary entries in voice over, the film dialectically montages two epochs, juxtaposing image and sound and bringing two distinct historical epochs into perspective.

Video reflexivity

The material form, the nonrealism of the imagery that video on mobile phones produces, was a significant reason for my use of the mobile phone in the making of *Moscow Diary*. The continued 'improvement' of video 'quality' on mobile phones works against this need in principle, though mobile phones will perhaps never match dedicated video cameras. The degraded image quality (degraded by whose standards?), grainy with blotchy coloring, with poor quality sound, is a decision that I made in order to foreground the technology, one that has been fairly common in experimental filmmaking, in particular structuralist filmmaking. In point of fact the image materiality, one that reveals to a certain extent, its technological production, is a 'thinking-form', denying the spectator an over-riding absorption and creating an open aesthetic that directly engages the spectator. The image, as Stiegler might say, is encased within a temporal technology.

The event

Which brings me to the idea of technics and the digital as a tool that can be used both by the powers-that-be, and those concerned with under-mining authority. Besides the isolated self-absorption and the avoidance of boredom and animal-like captivity that the mobile phone promotes, it has also been indispensible to direct action groups and many other political demonstrators, not too mention the rioters on London's streets in the summer of 2011. In fact one could characterize the mobile phone as an inherent part of the *event*, as theorized by Alain Badiou. Badiou's event occurs outside of the known, expected, or predicted. It is typically portrayed as a significant social and political rupture and break with

DOI: 10.1057/9781137469816.0008

authority, such as the Paris Commune or May 1968, but it can also be highly individualized and personal, such as falling in love. 'The most profound philosophical concepts tell us something like this: "If you want your life to have some meaning, you must accept the event, you must remain at distance from power, and you must be firm in your decision"' (Badiou and Zizek 2010, 13). The event is a situation that is unpredictable and outside of any truth-bearing definitions or theory, '... which compels us to decide a new way of being' (Badiou 2002, 41). The 'event' in Badiou's terms, is something unexpected, is hard to categorize and is tied to a kind of zeitgeist. The mobile phone can be used as an inherent part of the event. It can take on a role for the multiple, for the crowd who gathers to act against the system with all its controlling and policing mechanisms, and its attempts to put the lid on any semblance of spontaneous dissent or protest.

Discrete but infinite form

In Stiegler's essay, *The Discrete Image*, he proposes the view that the digital can take on a positive role and counter the industrial technological control of time and the image. On the one hand Stiegler, by reminding us that the 'mental is ephemeral' (2002, 155), so that we rely on technics of the image to preserve memory, recalls Roland Barthes's essay on the photograph, its bond with the indexical and the real of the *punctum*. On the other hand, the digital foregrounds the question of whether the image has ever truly existed. This is because manipulation is the essence of the digital—its pixelated structure—and this undermines our understanding of the indexicality of the image. The 'spectrum of continuity' (155) that the analog photograph retained with the indexical is broken. And so the awareness that the spectator has of the degree that the digital can be manipulated is empowering for, 'By discretizing the continuous, digitisation allows us to submit the this was to a *decomposing* analysis' (158). Furthermore, Stiegler claims the spectator is now engaged with a new cognizance, the chance to 'develop a culture of reception' (163). The spectator approaches the production of the digital produced image with an added dose of scepticism—but then, Stiegler fails to see that this is what experimental and structuralist films, challenging the temporal and spatial organization in mainstream cinema, were doing long before the digital came into being. As were those filmmakers and theorists who

DOI: 10.1057/9781137469816.0008

foregrounded the centrality of the filmic long take partly in order to challenge the 'artificiality' of Hollywood and further the transformative potential of cinema.

The film theorist André Bazin is best known for consistently arguing for the ontological status of cinema, which can convey the ambiguity of everyday reality through the long take and the deep focus shot. Although the long take cannot take the place of the event, as Bazin might have liked, it can reveal a reorientation of a group of people, actively contributing to the turn of events on an ongoing, day-to-day basis. The long take with its claims on authenticity and the real, rendered ever more dubious in the epoch of the digital and computer-generated images (CGI), is now utilized by those engaged in protests around the world, as a local and a global tool for collective participation, embedded in the event itself in its originary indexical state.

Crowd scenes, protests and violence are now captured in long take on mobile devices and cameras and uploaded to social media transmitted globally as ongoing evidence filmed in real time. Obviously the need for urgency and the difficulties of accessing editing software contribute to the fact that much of this footage has been conveyed in single takes without a commentary or voice over. Two minutes long, *Syria Assad Drops Explosive Barrel Bombs on Jabal Al Turkman* provides an example of the digital long take. It is an urgent communiqué to the outside world, and a reminder of the 'relationship between total artifice and total reality' (Badiou 2013, 233). In real time a two-minute mobile phone video records the bombing of Syrian city in two takes, each a minute long. As the camera point toward the blue sky, picking out a helicopter, gazing over the cityscape, across a hazy sea shouts of 'Allahu akbar!' ('God is great') are heard. The camera films continually, every explosion is accompanied by a sad, melancholic rendering of 'Allahu akbar!' and a short Arabic prayer.

Syria Assad Drops Explosive Barrel Bombs on Jabal Al Turkman reveals unpredictable history in the making, '... as if it were unwinding the spool of time' (Badiou 2013, 212). This 'being-there' of the digital footage, the 'digital real' one might say, paradoxically made possible by the digital as a discrete but infinite form, is largely undermined when it's shown on television news. Edited with a commentator's voice added, often shown with the proviso that the footage might not be what it claimed having been impossible to verify, making it something a lot more controlled,

DOI: 10.1057/9781137469816.0008

informational and distant. Then again, as time passes, the archival nature of this footage comes to the fore, although its original immediacy remains apparent, and utilizing Badiou's theory of the event, its futural openness preserved.

In a singular image, Gecko exposes the mobile phone as an object of desire, both a machine providing us with a kind of mastery over the world and a fetish that obscures us from the world. The mobile phone forms an inherent part of our global neo-liberal world, increasingly exploitative of people and the environment, increasingly fluid and spatially compressed, but one that allows itself to be used against the system and expose authority and power to global scrutiny. Like desire and its role in the unconscious the mobile phone short-circuits language, repressing memory in the act of forgetting what we cannot remember. It allows us to imagine that we are part of the flow of everyday life, prevents as feeling any sort of distance and lack, an imagined control for sure. But, as argued by Stiegler in particular, it is our awareness of technics, of the continual and ongoing relationship between the organic and the inorganic that can counter the 'corporate soul' of smartphone technology, and go against the flow and control of that which obscures itself behind a veil of mastery.

References

Agamben, Giorgio. 2004. *The Open, Man and Animal*, Trans. Kevin Attell. California: Stanford University Press.

Badiou, Alain. 2002. *Ethics: An Essay on the Understanding of Evil*. London: Verso.

Badiou, Alain. 2013. *Cinema*. Cambridge: Polity Press.

Badiou, Alain and Slavoj Zizek. 2009. *Philosophy in the Present*, trans. Cambridge: Polity.

Benjamin, Walter, *Moscow Diary*, October 35, Winter 1985, Massachusetts: MIT Press.

Bradley, Arthur. 2011. *Originary Technicity, The Theory of Technology from Marx to Derrida.*Basingstoke: Palgrave Macmillan.

Stiegler, Bernard. 2003. 'Our Ailing Educational Institutions', *Culture Machine* 5. http://www.culturemachine.net/index.php/cm/article/viewarticle/258/243

DOI: 10.1057/9781137469816.0008

Stiegler, Bernard. 2002. 'The Discrete Image'. *In Echographies of Television.* Trans. Jennifer Bajorek, Cambridge: Polity Press.

Stiegler, Bernard. 2010. *For a New Critique of Political Economy.* Cambridge: Polity Press.

DOI: 10.1057/9781137469816.0008

Part II
Space and Place

Berry, Marsha and Max Schleser. *Mobile Media Making in an Age of Smartphones.* New York: Palgrave Macmillan, 2014. DOI: 10.1057/9781137469816.0009.

▶

Telecommunications infrastructure has changed our environments in both visible and invisible ways. The invisible signals emitted from mobile phone towers, wifi modems, and smartphones are meshed with the physical landscape and are a part of the very air we breathe in our cities. The assemblages and configurations of mobile technology have irrevocably changed the ways in which we interact with each other and how we organize our days in the smartphone age. Smartphones also have had a significant impact on how we perceive place and have extended ways in which we may express our embodied interactions with and through places we traverse on a daily basis. Location-based media is now ubiquitous so we can readily let people know exactly where we are if we choose to do so.

Invisible co-present others have become an ambient fixture of everyday life through text messaging, social media, and networked games. New kinds of co-presence are emerging where online and offline cartographies have become meshed together. Pink and Hjorth (2012) frame this phenomenon as 'a shift from networked visuality to emplaced visuality and sociality' (145). The politics of mobile media of moving in and through space in an age of pervasive geospatial media has enormous implications and requires us to extend and expand the ways in which we think about nature of space and place.

The chapters in this section share a focus on how mobile technologies help us rethink space and place and the opportunities these new understandings provide for creative practice. They engage with debates concerning co-presence, embodied phenomena, and temporality as well as shifting networked socialities. Hjorth, Berry, and House engage with the notion that playing games, sharing photographs, and sending text messages through mobile media can have consequences in the physical world and provide opportunities for artists to intervene in urban spaces in tangible, evocative and sometimes surprising ways.

Digital ethnographic methodologies underpin the research presented in the chapters by both Hjorth and Berry. The relationship between online and offline socialities provides a lens through which the movements across places, temporalities including timezones and spaces are analyzed. Current debates and conceptualizations of space and place with regard to the impact of mobile and social media have shifted from dichotomies of anthropological place and nonplace as theorized by Augé (1995) to include a more holistic approach, which includes the entanglements of embodied and temporal relations. Massey argues that a progressive

DOI: 10.1057/9781137469816.0009

understanding of place should embrace both the global and the local where place becomes a dynamic process that may be 'conceptualized in terms of the social interactions which they tie together' (Massey 1994, 7). Space and place, then are not static entities, rather they are unbounded, dynamic, specific, and transitional from one state to the next.

What emerges from the research presented by Hjorth and Berry is that mobile technologies help us to rethink space and place in a way that tacks between local detail and global structures 'in such as way as to bring them into simultaneous view' (Geertz 1983, 68). What emerges from their research is that space and place are networked, embodied, emotional, playful, and messy. They are simultaneously global with local nuances and in a constant state of motion.

House approaches the question of how smartphones encourage us to rethink space and place through arts based practice. He argues that despite the rapid advances of smartphones and location-based media, SMS remains a fertile field for creative practices that offer alternative ways of rethinking space and place which participate in the traditions of the psychogeography of Guy Debord and the 1960s Fluxus movement. His chapter provides a historical perspective on space and place that engages with contemporary debates and theoretical frames in the creative arts.

References

Augé, Marc. 1995. *Non-Places: Introduction to an Anthropology of Supermodernity*. London: Verso.

Geertz, Clifford. 1983. 'From the Native's Point of View: On the Nature of Anthropological Understanding', in *Local Knowledge: Further Essays in Interpretative Anthropology*. New York: Basic Books, 55–72.

Massey, Doreen. 1994. 'A Global Sense of Place.' http://www.aughty.org/pdf/global_sense_place.pdf, 1–8 (accessed June 28, 2014).

Pink, Sarah and Larissa Hjorth. 2012. 'Emplaced Cartographies: Reconceptualising camera phone practices in an age of locative media', *Media International Australia* 145: 145–156.

DOI: 10.1057/9781137469816.0009

5

Co-present and Ambient Play: A Case Study of Mobile Gaming

Larissa Hjorth

Abstract: *From Tetris and Angry Birds to location-based services multi-player games like Ingress, what constitutes mobile gaming has changed dramatically. In these various modalities and affordances, there is a multiplicity of engagement, distraction, and embodiment that cannot be encompassed by the outdated notion of 'casual' play. Mobile games are often described as casual—a label that camouflages the different modes of engagement, labor, and embodiment. In this chapter two key concepts informing contemporary mobile gaming are discussed. A site-specific mobile game (keitai mizu [mobile water]) made for a Tokyo post 3/11 tsunami and Fukushima disaster is presented to illustrate the concepts.* Keitai mizu *renders players into investigators by uncovering the natural water streams under the urban cartographies.*

Berry, Marsha and Max Schleser. *Mobile Media Making in an Age of Smartphones.* New York: Palgrave Macmillan, 2014. DOI: 10.1057/9781137469816.0010.

DOI: 10.1057/9781137469816.0010

From *Tetris* and *Angry Birds* to location-based service (LBS) multi-player games like *Ingress,* mobile gaming has changed dramatically in an age of smartphones. In these various modalities and affordances, we can see a multiplicity of engagement, distraction and embodiment that cannot be encompassed by the outdated notion of 'casual' play (Juul 2009; Taylor 2012). Site-specific mobile games can help to uncover psychological, playful, and emotional dimensions of place. Moreover, with the rise in gamified LBS like *Foursquare* and China's *Jiepang,* the unofficial role of camera phone practices becomes central. Camera phone practices highlight the need to understand everyday life as a series of movements across places, spaces and temporalities. Camera phone photo taking and sharing can be viewed as part of ambient play as well as intimate co-presence. Camera phone practices not only interweave play with sociality in creative ways but are also a key sense-making tool for understanding two key factors in mobile gaming beyond the casual: *ambient play* and *intimate co-presence.*

Ambient play contextualizes the game within broader processes of sociality and embodied media practices, and is essential to the corporeality of play (Bayliss 2007; Dourish 2001) whereby play in, and outside, the game space reflects broader cultural nuances and phenomena. As Bayliss argues, there is a need to address specific modes of embodiment within gameplay. Bayliss turns to the work of HCI (Human Computer Interaction) expert Paul Dourish (2001) in regards to embodied interaction. As Bayliss states, 'gameplay is an embodied phenomenon, one that can only exist as experienced by the player situated in the particular context of their own experience' (2007: 1). Moving beyond the counterproductive ludology versus narratology debate underlining early game studies debates, Bayliss utilizes Katie Salen and Eric Zimmerman's definition of gameplay as the 'formalized interaction' that happens when players follow game rules through the experience of play (2004). According to Bayliss, Dourish's notion of embodied play is particularly useful to understanding gameplay, that is, its 'not that it is a particular form of gameplay that is embodied, but instead it is an approach to gameplay that sees embodiment as a central, and essential part of the wider phenomenon' (2007, 4).

In this chapter, I will discuss these two key concepts—*ambient play* and *intimate co-presence*—informing contemporary mobile gaming and then discuss a site-specific mobile game (*keitai mizu* [mobile water]) made for a Tokyo post 3/11 tsunami and Fukushima disaster context. *Keitai mizu*

DOI: 10.1057/9781137469816.0010

renders players into investigators by using the camera phone and Twitter as part of the discovery process in uncovering the natural water streams under the urban cartographies. So let us begin with setting the context.

Tokyo post 3/11

When the earthquake occurred, I was alone in my room playing a monster hunter PSP (Playstation Portable) game. Exactly at the time, I was fighting with a monster who makes an earthquake so that I did not realize that an actual, offline quake had occurred. Only after beating down the monster, I realized something different around me. A fish tank had overflowed and books had fallen down. Initially I was not really shocked by the earthquake itself, but felt frustration with the aftermath—the power failure, panic buying, nuclear accident, and such stuff. During this time I stayed inside with a friend and continued to play the monster hunter game. But the game was no longer entertaining ('Toshi', 25 Japanese male).

The quote from 'Toshi' sees him playing a haptic game during the 2011 Tokyo earthquake, tsunami and earthquake disaster known as 3/11. Affective and personal technologies such as social and mobile media make us rethink old psychological models of emotion. In times of trauma, mobile media are increasingly becoming a vehicle for material and immaterial textures and contours of grief. Everybody deals with crisis in different ways, and this individualism is being amplified within mobile media just as it is creating new avenues for accessing a sense of community, support, and help.

Toshi's immersion within the PSP game was so deep that he mistook the quake vibrations for the monster's movements within his game. In the moments after he realized the horror of real life event, he desperately tried to contract friends and family but to no avail. In the days after 3/11 and as multiple and conflicting news reports emerged across mass and social media, Toshi with a friend used the game to hide from the pain and confusion. Later as it emerged that the national broadcaster, NHK, had deliberately withheld important information about the Fukushima reactor under the instructions of the government.

Toshi is not unique. Like millions of other Japanese he shifted his trust toward mobile media like Twitter and LBS like Foursquare and Instagram not only to gain a sense of intimate publics but also to have a sense of perpetual co-presence with his family and friends. What becomes

DOI: 10.1057/9781137469816.0010

apparent in conversation with Toshi is his gameplay is about intentional escapism, particularly when the world is too traumatic and confusing. The picture that begins to emerge is one whereby there are multiple forms of presence and engagement around mobile gaming that needs to be accounted for beyond the clumsy notion of casual game play.

As noted elsewhere, mobile games are often problematically categorized as casual games (Hjorth 2008)—but as Keogh notes, 'a casual game does not simply offer an easier or more shallow experience than a traditional videogame, but an experience that is more flexible with the player's time, more easily incorporated into the player's everyday life' (Keogh 2014, n.p). It is this flexibility and ease of incorporation, especially when adapted to mobile social media games or involving the insinuation of game elements into an application or service, that so thoroughly instills mobile games into the routines and habits of our social lives. One way to understand mobile games beyond the problematic label of casual is through ambient play and intimate co-presence.

Connecting co-presence with ambient play

Literature around co-presence within mobile communication fields has flourished with the work of Christian Licoppe and Mizuko Ito as a productive way for rethinking traditional binaries that are no longer adequate in everyday life. Binaries such as here and there, virtual and actual, online and offline, absent and present have been eroded through media practices such as mobile media. The rubric of co-presence provides a broader context for understanding intimacy and mediation as something that is not only a late 20th or 21st century phenomenon but also as something that has been an integral part of being social and human.

With the rise in computer-related disciplines such as Human Computer Interaction (HCI) and mobile media, presence has again taken on a heightened importance to describe various states of embodiment and engagement across multiple platforms, screens, and contexts. Broadly defined, in the present context, co-presence can be understood as referring to:

[T]he degree to which geographically dispersed agents experience a sense of physical and/or psychological proximity through the use of particular communication technologies (Milne 2010, 165).

DOI: 10.1057/9781137469816.0010

As Giuseppe Mantovani and Giuseppe Riva (1998) have noted, early debates in internet studies failed to acknowledge that 'presence is always mediated' and that it is culturally constructed. And yet, equally significant is recognizing that 'the ability of the subject to elide or ignore this mediation is crucial to the presence effect' (Milne 2010, 165). It is in this way that presence can be been understood as a psychological state whereby some form of technology has shaped subjective experience and perception.

The concept of co-presence deliberately conceives of presence as a spectrum of engagement across multiple pathways of connection—and thus goes beyond counter-productive dichotomous models of online and offline, here and there, virtual and actual. The concept also allows us to connect the contemporary with the historical in terms of the evolution of mediated intimacies. As Ingrid Richardson notes,

The 'sensing' of mobile communication and interactive media elicits an intimately audio, visual, sometimes haptic, 'handy' and visceral awareness, a mode of embodiment which demands the ontological coincidence of distance and closeness, presence and telepresence, actual and virtual (Richardson 2005, n.p.).

Another way in which camera phones demonstrate both *remediated* and *emergent* modes within mobile games is through ambient play. While mobile media remediates—that is, remixes old and new media in cyclic ways (Bolter and Grusin 1999)—it also shapes and is shaped by the overlay between the social and creative. Ambience is often used to describe sound and music but has also been used in computing and science. As a noun, it specifically refers to a style of music with electronic textures and no consistent beat that is used to create a mood or feeling, but more generally the term describes the diffuse atmosphere of a place—an affective texture of place. In short, ambience is about the texture of context, emotion, and affect. Ambient play is a more useful rubric for understanding mobile gaming's diverse experiences of embodiment and distraction beyond the problematic label of 'casual' (Hjorth and Richardson 2014).

In my *keitai mizu* project I deployed the concepts of *intimate co-presence* and *ambient play* by recruiting the significant role of camera phone taking and sharing within Japanese everyday practices. My ARC Linkage project entitled *Spatial Dialogues* was motivated by the question: how could we harness Twitter and camera phone apps to make a game that reflected upon the environment in new ways? It was in a post 3/11 context that collaborations with Japanese artists and activists for this project began.

DOI: 10.1057/9781137469816.0010

Keitai mizu: a site-specific mobile game

Through a series of video, sound, game, and sculptural narratives *SHIBUYA: UNDERGROUND STREAMS* sought to make the general public in Tokyo consider the underground streams making up much of Tokyo. In particular, the project focused upon one of the busiest places in the world, Shibuya. By placing a shipping container in a park over the month of June, the project sought to explore the idea of cartographies—water, emotional, social, playful, psychological, historical, and geographic. Given that Tokyo is made up of numerous little rivers underneath all the trains and roads we wanted to make audiences aware that they are literally perpetually *walking on water* (Figure. 5.1).

I asked Japanese and Australian artists to make a series of abstract and representational works of water creatures, which were then placed around the park. The project sought to disrupt dichotomies between art and nonart, water and nonwater, game and nongame, player and ethnographer. Players had 15 minutes to hunt for, photo and share online various *native-only* water-related creatures and objects that have been placed

FIGURE 5.1 *Shibuya: underground streams*

DOI: 10.1057/9781137469816.0010

around the site. They then 'captured' the art with their camera phones, and shared it online on Twitter or Instagram. Winners only sent pictures of the native species to the keitaimizu Twitter account (Figure 5.2). The game deployed both old (geocaching) and new (Twitter and Instagram) media to turn players into ethnographers.

The game space was blurred across online and offline spaces with Instagram and Twitter enabling co-present friends to share the experiences and images. Through the process of game play, participants became more mindful of the local water species as well as reflective upon the fact that the city is made up of numerous little rivers underneath all the trains and roads. We wanted to make audiences aware that they are literally perpetually *walking on water* (Figure 5.1).

FIGURE 5.2   Keitai mizu *(mobile water) game*

DOI: 10.1057/9781137469816.0010

FIGURE 5.3   Keitai mizu *players*

Keitai mizu attempted challenge boundaries between official and unofficial game spaces by blurring them with different modes of play (Figure 5.3). In particular, camera phone practices partake in new haptic visualities that bring emotional and social dimensions of place and play to the official game play space and drive the motivation for use. By deploying camera phone practices as part of the mobile game, players can develop the melodramatic elements—the affective and emotional dimensions—to engage friends into the play of being mobile.

Part of the enjoyment of the project was not only the entanglements between the methods and its transmission but also how the project lived on in different ways that saw the participants taking the key role. For example, when one student group came through to play, one of the other students took it on herself to document the their experiences and responses and turn it into a short film which she then uploaded onto video. This video was one of the few artifacts of transmission left after the ephemeral work had ceased. Moreover, traces of the play could be

DOI: 10.1057/9781137469816.0010

found in participants' twitter accounts, creating new nodes for co-present entanglement.

Conclusion: co-present and ambient play

In this chapter I have proposed an understanding of camera phone photography and Twitter micronarratives as an important part and yet often unofficial part of mobile gaming. Through the case study of *keitai mizu* I deployed camera phone apps and Twitter to consider the ways in which intimate co-presence and ambient play exists in, and around, mobile gaming within the everyday.

By deploying notions of ambient play and intimate co-presence I have sought to complicate the way in which mobile games are understood through the problematic label of casual play which camouflages the various forms of labor (time, financial, social, and emotional) involved. In exploring camera phone practices in relation to mobile gaming I have sought to bring camera phones' often unofficial role into the official space of gaming. Through the discussion of *keitai mizu*, I have sought to provide poetic ways in which players can become investigators in understanding their everyday environments in new ways.

References

Bayliss, Peter. 2007. 'Notes Toward a Sense of Embodied Gameplay', *DIGRA Conference,* June, Tokyo, http://lmc.gatech.edu/~cpearce3/ DiGRA07/Proceedings/013.pdf (accessed October 9, 2013).

Dourish, Paul. 2001. *Where the Action Is: The Foundations of Embodied Interaction.* Cambridge, MA: MIT Press.

Hjorth, Larissa. 2008. 'The Game of Being Mobile: One Media History of Gaming and Mobile Technologies in Asia-Pacific', *Convergence: The International Journal of Research into New Media Technologies* 13 (4): 369–381.

Hjorth, Larissa and Ingrid Richardson. 2014. *Gaming in Locative, Social and Mobile Media.* London: Palgrave.

Ito, Mizuko. 2003. 'Mobiles and the Appropriation of Place', *Receiver* 8, http://academic.evergreen.edu/curricular/evs/readings/itoShort.pdf (accessed December 10, 2005).

DOI: 10.1057/9781137469816.0010

Juul, Jesper. 2009. *A Casual Revolution: Reinventing Video Games and their Players*. Cambridge, MA: MIT Press.

Keitai mizu 2013. Available at: http://spatialdialogues.net/tokyo/ keitaimizu/, http://spatialdialogues.net/tokyo/live-in-tokyo/audience-response-to-shibuya-underground-streams/

Keogh, Brendan. 2014. 'Paying Attention to *Angry Birds:* Rearticulating Hybrid Worlds and Embodied Play through Casual iPhone Games', in G. Goggin and L. Hjorth (eds.), *Mobile Media Companion*. New York: Routledge, forthcoming.

Mantovani, Giovanni and Giovanni Riva. 1998. "Real' Presence: How Different Ontologies Generate Different Criteria for Presence, Telepresence and Virtual Presence', *Presence: Teleoperators and Virtual Environments* 1 (1): 540–550.

Richardson, Ingrid. 2005. 'Mobile Technosoma: Some Phenomenological Reflections on Itinerant Media Devices', *Fibreculture Journal* 6, http://six.fibreculturejournal.org/fcj-032-mobile-technosoma-some-phenomenological-reflections-on-itinerant-media-devices/ (accessed May 7, 2007).

Salen, Katie and Eric Zimmerman. 2004. *Rules of Play: Game Design Fundamentals*. Cambridge, MA: MIT Press.

Taylor, T. L. 2012. *Raising the Stakes: E-Sports and the Professionalization of Computer Gaming*. Cambridge, MA: MIT Press.

DOI: 10.1057/9781137469816.0010

6

Filtered Smartphone Moments: Haunting Places

Marsha Berry

Abstract: *People are endeavoring to capture more than an accurate depiction of what their eyes can see. Objects such as poems and photographs have become entangled in routine social interactions online. They are using faux-vintage filters on smartphone apps to go beyond visual sense to create a strong sense of place. The faux-vintage photography movement has strong resonances with the idea of hauntology, a concept coined by Derrida in Spectres de Marx (1993). This theoretical frame is used to situate this commonplace and creative practice within emergent socialities and visualities associated with social and mobile media. It is argued in this chapter that impulse to create and share a poetic and haunting image of a place can trigger social media smartphone camera moments.*

Berry, Marsha and Max Schleser. *Mobile Media Making in an Age of Smartphones.* New York: Palgrave Macmillan, 2014. DOI: 10.1057/9781137469816.0011.

DOI: 10.1057/9781137469816.0011

Jenny, a 60-something grandmother is in her garden in Wales chatting with a co-present friend who lives in the United States of America on Twitter. As she chats on her smartphone, she watches the way the light catches the wasps. She takes a picture, smiling because she knows how people react to wasps and takes a close-up picture of a wasp with Instagram. She uses a geo-tag to show her location because she wants people to know that the wasp is with her now, in her garden. She finds a filter that gives just the right sinister edge and posts it to Twitter. Responses quickly come from her followers along the lines of 'don't get stung' and 'ewww'. She shares the joke with her co-present friend who has joined in the playful banter on the timeline. She retorts in kind, 'haha, the wasps better watch out for me, I have a bigger sting'.

We are seeing new ways of using still and moving images, which are new types of 'emplaced visuality and geospatial sociality' (Pink and Hjorth 2012, 153) as soon as new camera phone applications such as EyeEm, Vine, and Instagram are released and taken up. Jenny loves socializing on Twitter and spends a large part of her days on social media as she is retired. She is a poet as well as a visual artist and enjoys writing haiga, a Japanese form of poetry where words and images are juxtaposed. She finds Twitter and Instagram ideal for this pursuit. Objects such as poems and photographs have become entangled in Jenny's routine social interactions online. She shares creative expressions alongside playful banter with friends and followers who are co-present through networked technology yet are physically absent.

In order to locate the haunted and emplaced visualities evident in social media within broader conceptualizations of place and space, I would like to elucidate how geographic place may be understood and how it is connected to social and creative practices. Massey (2005) theorizes space as inter-related flows, energies and the things it renders so that a place 'is always in the process of being made. It is never finished; never closed' (Massey 2005, 9) and we are always and already emplaced. The Hertzian space of flows, which may be defined as the electromagnetic telecommunications and wireless networking infrastructures present in urban environments (de Waal 2007) is also an integral part of many of our landscapes. Indeed, as Crang and Graham (2007) have argued, many landscapes have become sentient through the use of locative mobile technologies such as smartphones. Through these, a place enters into reflexive relations with its present and co-present inhabitants and these entangled relations constantly move in complex ways to generate new practices, socialities, and visualities.

DOI: 10.1057/9781137469816.0011

The landscape itself is not separate from us, rather is a 'region of the body's very existence, without which no knowing or remembering would be possible' (Ingold 2010, S122). We are meshed within the landscape and move through it. While it is impossible for a video or photograph to capture every aspect of any particular place, people are endeavoring to express what being in a place means to them by sharing video and photographs as a form of poetic spacing. Landscapes flow and change constantly with each addition and entanglement of networked technology, and we are all dynamic parts of our geographic places.

In this chapter, I explore the popularity of the use of faux-vintage smartphone camera apps to evoke analog effects. These practices are more than simple nostalgia. I use the frame of hauntology to situate this commonplace and creative practice within emergent socialities and visualities associated with mobile media. I contend that camera phone photographs and videos are emplaced dynamic images that show our desire to share corporeal connections to the weather-world (Ingold 2010) while socializing with co-present others and that faux-vintage apps are a part of this Gordian knot of contemporary socialities.

Following Pink and Hjorth's (2012) departure from the notion of 'ambient co-presence' (Okabe and Ito 2006), I will use their concept of 'emplaced visuality' to situate a contemporary understanding of smartphone camera practices and the socialities that both create and 'emerge through them' (Pink and Hjorth 2012, 145). This chapter focuses on a short digital ethnography of smartphone users who self-identify as creative artists. The study was conducted over a two-month period in 2013 and comprised sixteen semi-structured interviews with participants from the USA, UK, Holland, and Australia as well as online observation. Interestingly, each of the respondents reported that smartphones made art practices more accessible and routine for them.

Shifting practices

Where once most amateur movies and photographs were associated with the capture of special occasions and family archives (Hirsch, 1997), they are now enmeshed in a myriad of practices associated with networked information and communication technology (ICT) assemblages and affordances we refer to as Web 2.0 and social media (Gibson 1979/1986; Gómez Cruz and Meyer 2012; Soegaard 2003). Some earlier studies of digital and camera

DOI: 10.1057/9781137469816.0011

phone photography (Gye 2007; Okabi and Ito 2006; Van House et al. 2004) focused on the uses of mobile phone photography as technologies of the self. Indeed Gye proposed, 'the kinds of photos that are most often taken with mobile camera phones are those that reinforce the user's individuality rather than their ties to other groups' (Gye 2007, 284).

Jenny's use of photos outlined above suggests that there has been considerable evolution in practices since Gye's (2007) observations. This is further supported by information supplied by Wendy who is in her early thirties. Photos play a large role in her online social spaces—her friends and colleagues comment on each other's photos a lot. She takes photos of people because she is a people person but she also loves her part of the world so she often takes photos of the ever-changing sea-view as well to share her sense of place.

The convergence of smart phone cameras and networked technology is creating new socio-technical communication environments where the production and the distribution of visual images are now commonplace in social media networks. An approach based on the analysis of everyday practices known as the 'practice turn' (Cetina et al. 2001) provides a lens through which everyday activities may be understood, including creative practices. The ability to experiment with the look of photographs and video is readily accessible to everyone who has a smartphone. Kelly, a photographer and street artist enjoys the ease of Instagram and posts photos of things she finds interesting or inspiring about 15 times a day to Instagram and Twitter. She has 27 photo apps on her smartphone and uses seven on a daily basis. She likes apps that have good filters and editing tools. Clearly, we no longer need sophisticated 'expertise in computer post-processing software', as Gómez Cruz and Meyer (2012, 216) have pointed out.

Haunted by faux-vintage apps

As stated earlier, I want to explore the proposition that camera phone photographs and videos are dynamic images that show footprints in the open world (Ingold 2008) haunted by more than the nostalgia of analog aesthetics. As well as evoking the sensation of moving through a specific place, many images that seek to capture and interpret a moment in time as a *lieux de memoiré* (Nora 1989) are often haunted by a desire to show some continuity with the past. However there is a

DOI: 10.1057/9781137469816.0011

paradox here. Nora points to a rupture between memory and history that is widening due to the forces of globalization and migration, and aggravated by 'our hopelessly forgetful modern societies, propelled by change' (1989, 8). Yet social media and emplaced visualities are providing us with ways of assuaging our thirst for continuity. Palmer suggests 'a dynamic visual timeline enables users to supplement their own photographic memories with fragments from the mass media, thereby aiding memorialization and personalizing history' (Palmer 2010, 155) and filters that refer to analog affects can serve this urge to be part of the stream of history.

I have noticed that numerous images shared on social media referring to particular places participate in a faux-vintage photography movement (Schutt and Berry 2012). I contend that this has resonance with the idea of hauntology, a concept coined by Derrida in *Spectres de Marx* (1993). Derrida refers to the specter as a cipher for the unsettling of the present by unresolved, repressed, or malevolent aspects of the past. Co-presence can be spectral, dislocating, and unsettling. The participants in my ethnography reported experiencing this directly when they converse with people residing in different time zones whereby clock-time is no longer assumed to be shared.

Hauntology as a concept has travelled widely through disciplines and used in various ways. For example, pre-Raphaelite art movement expresses spectral qualities whereby the nostalgic medieval aesthetics of artists such as Gabriel Rossetti may be interpreted as symptomatic of anxieties about modernity and the industrial age. Gallix provides a very useful commentary about this concept in an article published in the Guardian in 2011. Gallix argues that 'hauntology is, above all, the product of a time which is seriously "out of joint" where "new technologies are dislocating more traditional notions of time and place' and they 'encourage us never to fully commit to the here and now, fostering a ghostly presence-absence and furthermore, that hauntology 'is not just a symptom of the times...it is itself haunted by a nostalgia for all our lost futures' (Gallix 2011, n.p.).

Networked media has accelerated the pace of our lives—the participants in my digital ethnography reported that while they enjoyed their newfound forms of networked sociality all 16 wished they could have more down time not connected to social media. Indeed one participant called Will, who relished the aesthetic opportunities of faux-vintage photo apps gave him, said that he was avoiding exploring video apps because he

DOI: 10.1057/9781137469816.0011

found social media so enjoyable he felt he needed to place boundaries to prevent him from spending too much time on it at the expense of other necessary daily routines. He also expressed nostalgia for the presocial media days when he felt he had more control over the demands on his time and felt freer to commit to new pursuits. Yet at the same time he said he wouldn't be without the creative opportunities the world social media had shown him and access to the kindred spirits he had met on Twitter.

Smartphones have irrevocably altered and unsettled our sense of place as well as of time. They can encourage people's dislocation from physical surroundings. We walk along streets and paths oblivious to our physical surroundings because we are immersed in the contents of our smartphone screens. Face-to-face encounters are disrupted frequently by the spectral co-presence of others. This, in turn, fosters widespread nostalgia for a lost future where there is no pressure or temptation to be constantly connected via networked technology. The corollary of this is a yearning to be more closely connected in a visceral way to the places we pass through on a daily basis. We are also haunted by a lost future where we can be in a place without the unsettling specters of co-present others just about everywhere we go. It is quite possible that the popularity of faux-vintage apps is both symptomatic of our times and a product of hauntology.

The impulse to create a poetic image of a sense of place triggers social media smartphone camera moments. These visual practices have become routine and are entangled in the evolving socialities of social media, which are growing exponentially. For example, there are over 150 million people using Instagram as reported on their blog September 9, 2013, which represents a growth of over +900% since Instagram's inception in October 2010 (http://nitrogr.am/instagram-statistics/). The Instagram platform may be regarded as a giant and messy archive (Cresswell 2012) that includes a myriad of poetic *lieux de memoiré* documenting emplaced visuality.

The popularity of faux-vintage apps such as Instagram indicates that people are endeavoring to capture more than an accurate depiction of what their eyes can see. They are using analog aesthetics to go beyond visual sense to interpret aspects of sensory experiences in order to create an atmospheric sense of place. A blog post by John Constine, a technology journalist for Tech Crunch, may be seen as evidence of this emergent form of visuality. He describes his first Instagram photo sharing

DOI: 10.1057/9781137469816.0011

experience. What is of note here, is the urge to create a poetic moment of being in a landscape through the use of a camera app filter:

> But my most vivid 'eureka' moment with social media happened while I was walking in Golden Gate Park at sunset. Before me, creamy cloudflare reflected off a pond. It was so beautiful it felt selfish to keep it to myself. I wanted all my friends to see what I saw.
>
> But I was no photographer, and held just a crummy early-generation iPhone. The shot lacked the vibrance and emotion of being there. Yet with Instagram's filters I could return the essence of the moment to what I captured with my camera. And with time, a community grew around the ability to be transported. (Constine 2013, n.p.)

The urge to communicate a multisensorial essence of place is reminiscent of Lyotard's somewhat romantic understanding of place and landscape. In his essay 'Scapeland', Lyotard sketches a notion of landscape, which engages the whole sensorium: landscape becomes a 'vanishing of a standpoint' through 'an excess of presence' (Lyotard 1989, 216). A corporeal connection to place can also be a key factor in the urge to share still and moving images through social media apps as Constine's (2013) column shows and is reflective of our very human need to communicate experiences we find significant in some way to each other.

The need to share routine yet significant connections to places is evident in John's creative and social practices with his smartphone. He reported that he photographed a pair of swans raising signets over a three-month period and posted these to his Twitter feed each day. He walked along the path beside the canal in the south of England where the swans lived each day on his way to the bus stop. This was a precious part of his day because he was free of the pressure to be connected to email, etc. He wanted to communicate his need to be corporeally immersed in commonplace sights, sounds, and sensations that were integral to his creative practice. He used filters to evoke what it was like to be there, fully present, each day. One could argue that our desire to be haunted by the look and ambience of analog media is symptom matic our unresolved relationships with our new technologies, including our smartphones.

Haunting places

As already mentioned, most camera apps for have an array of filters to add atmospheric effects evoking analog technology. Many of these

DOI: 10.1057/9781137469816.0011

filters reproduce the look of heritage media such as Super 8 movies, lomography, and black and white film. I conclude that the popularity of filters to add a poetic dimension to photographs and video shot on a camera phone is reflective of a desire to evoke the corporeal aspects of being in a place including the weather, the smells and textures of the scene and/or events (Ingold 2010), emotional states and the sense of comfort or otherwise that this brings. Photography has thus moved beyond a representation of what is before the eyes to evoke and communicate the physical sensations of being emplaced (Figure 6.1).

The sheer volume of videos uploaded each day to social media sites such as Twitter, Facebook, Instagram, Vine show how commonplace our shared expressions of our footprints in the weather-world (Ingold

FIGURE 6.1   *Being haunted in suburbia*

DOI: 10.1057/9781137469816.0011

2010) really are. These expressions of emplaced visuality are an emerging vernacular. As Gómez Cruz and Meyer (2012) have declared, the smartphone moment is the fifth moment of photography; and it has arrived. Through the examples of practices from my ethnography with smartphone cameras, I have presented some of the ways we might seek to understand the popularity of faux-vintage apps in a way that goes beyond nostalgia and analog aesthetics. We need to also account for the unsettling and spectral affects of co-presence and how locative social media enacts and re-enacts emplaced visualities and in turn how these practices are shaping and challenging our normative aesthetics with regard to photography and video.

References

Constine, John. 2013. 'Instagram, Technology's Window To The Soul', TechCrunch, retrieved from http://techcrunch.com/2013/06/20/to-thee-i-do-commend-my-watchful-soul-ere-i-let-fall-the-windows-of-mine-eyes/ (accessed September 19, 2013).

Crang, Michael andStephen Graham. 2007. 'Sentient Cities: Ambient Intelligence and the Politics of Urban Space', *Information, Communication and Society* 10: 789–817.

Cresswell, Tim. 2012. 'Value, Gleaning and the Archive at Maxwell Street, Chicago', *Transactions of the Institute of British Geographers* 37(1): 164–176.

Derrida, Jacques. 1993. *Specters of Marx: the state of the debt, the Work of Mourning, & the New International*. Oxford: Routledge.

de Waal, Martijin. 2007. 'No more Bowling Alone? Locative Media and Urban Culture', in Locative Media Summer Conference. Siegen: Museum of Contemporary Art.

Gallix, Andrew. 2011. 'Hauntology: A not-so-new critical manifestation', *The Guardian Newspaper*, retrieved from http://www.theguardian.com/books/booksblog/2011/jun/17/hauntology-critical (accessed September 19, 2013).

Gibson, James, J. 1979/1986. *The Ecological Approach to Visual Perception*. Hillsdale, NJ: Lawrence Erlbaum Associates.

Gómez Cruz, Edgar and Eric T. Meyer. 2012. 'Creation and Control in the Photographic Process: iPhones and the emerging fifth moment of photography', *Photographies* 5 (2): 203–221.

DOI: 10.1057/9781137469816.0011

Gye, Lisa. 2007. 'Picture This: the Impact of Mobile Camera Phones on Personal Photographic Practices', *Continuum: Journal of Media and Cultural Studies* 21 (2): 279–288.

Hirsch, Marianne. 1997. *Family Frames: Photography, Narrative and Postmemory.* Cambridge, MA: Harvard UP.

Ingold, Tim. 2008. 'Bindings Against Boundaries: Entanglements of Life in an Open World', *Environment and Planning A* 40(8): 1796–1810.

Ingold, Tim. 2010. 'Footprints Through the Weather-World: Walking, Breathing, Knowing', *Journal of the Royal Anthropological Institute* (N. S.): S121–S139.

Lyotard, Jean-Francois. 1989. *The Lyotard Reader.* Oxford: Basil Blackwell.

Massey, Doreen. 2005. *For Space*, London: Sage.

Nora, Pierre. 1989. 'Between Memory and History: Les lieux de memoire', *Representations* 26: 7–24.

Okabe, D and M. Ito. 2006. 'Everyday Contexts of Camera Phone Use: Steps Toward Technosocial Ethnographic Frameworks', in J. Hofflich and M. Hartmann (eds), *Mobile Communication in Everyday Life: an Ethnographic View.* Berlin: Frank and Timm.

Palmer, Daniel. 2010. 'Emotional Archives: Online Photo Sharing and the Cultivation of the Self', *Photographies* 3 (2): 155–171.

Pink, Sarah and Larissa Hjorth. 2012. 'Emplaced Cartographies: Reconceptualising Camera Phone Practices in an Age of Locative Media', *Media International Australia*, 145: 145–156.

Soegaard, Mads. 2003. 'Affordances', retrieved 22 July 2013 from http://www.interaction-design.org/encyclopedia/affordances.html.

Van House, Nancy A., Marc Davis, Yuri Takhteyev, Morgan Ames, and Megan Finn. 2004. The social uses of personal photography: methods for projecting future imaging applications, retrieved from http://people.ischool.berkeley.edu/~vanhouse/van%20house_et_al_2004b%20.pdf (accessed September 20, 2013).

DOI: 10.1057/9781137469816.0011

7

Subversive Mobile Storytelling

Brian House

Abstract: *This chapter proposes that SMS (Short Message Service) text-messaging on mobile devices can serve as a narrative medium that subverts traditional boundaries of the experience of literature. In a world of increasingly rich media, text has retained its significance on mobile devices through such emerging forms as the SMS novel. The nature of a mobile device used in an urban environment also invokes the Situationist International's concern with the subjectivity of place, which has been a point of departure for the discussion of locative media. Further, the imperative poetics of text-messaging suggest its use as a contemporary tool in the kind of nontheatrical performance envisioned by Fluxus, a use demonstrated by Tim Etchell's Surrender Control. Uniquely positioned to combine these methodologies, SMS allows the transposition of literature into the experiential domain, animating fictional text with everyday life. An original artwork, The Wrench, is presented as an example.*

Berry, Marsha and Max Schleser. *Mobile Media Making in an Age of Smartphones.* New York: Palgrave Macmillan, 2014. DOI: 10.1057/9781137469816.0012.

DOI: 10.1057/9781137469816.0012

SMS (Short Message Service) text-messaging on mobile devices can serve as a narrative medium that subverts traditional boundaries of the experience of literature. In a world of increasingly rich media, text has retained its significance on mobile devices through such emerging forms as the SMS novel, yet much of its potential remains untapped. As an interface to a computer system, SMS can serve as a medium for what Espen Aarseth has dubbed 'cybertext', in which narrative is produced through the process of interactive feedback. Additionally, the imperative poetics of text-messaging suggest its use in a contemporary form of the nontheatrical performance envisioned by Fluxus. Uniquely positioned to combine these methodologies, SMS allows the transposition of literature into the experiential domain, animating fictional text with everyday life. An original artwork, The Wrench, is presented as an example.

Technically, the SMS is embedded in the signaling mechanism of cellular networks that routes voice calls, and so in some sense is a medium that is more fundamental to the mobile phone than audio (Hillebrand 2001, 414). Though SMS was not envisioned as a consumer service, in 2006 about 43 billion messages were sent on New Year's Eve alone (Vnunet 2008), indicating that text-messaging has become one of the dominant communication technologies of our time.

Most SMS messages make no pretense to literary grandeur. The medium's minimalism can be dramatically suggestive, however—consider, for example, the 'Leila Texts'. Due to a glitch in the network of the mobile operator Verizon, all messages addressed to the handle 'Leila' were for a time mistakenly sent to a woman from Brooklyn named Leila Sales, though they may have been intended for other Leilas. Sales runs a blog in which she attempts to interpret the drama behind the messages:

> Lst ngt was… weird. im sorry. pls dont tell her.
>
> from a 914 phone number, Tuesday, March 4, 1:47 PM
>
> This text is absolutely rife with possibilities … I don't think that 914 guy drunkenly made out with Leila, even though he has a girlfriend. While that could explain 'Lst ngt was… weird,' as well as 'pls dont tell her' (i.e. 'my girlfriend'), 'im sorry' wouldn't really make sense there. Unless he drunkenly made out with Leila AGAINST LEILA'S WILL, in which case my explanation could work. Alternate explanations, please? (Sales 2008)

Sales often responds to the messages, offering her unsolicited advice to the unsuspecting sender, despite her inevitable misreadings. Arguably,

DOI: 10.1057/9781137469816.0012

the ambiguities of the fragments suggest more than what might be said in a richer medium.

In fact, text-messaging has given rise to a new genre, that of the SMS novel. Popular largely in China and Japan, the text is delivered in two daily instalments consisting of a message each. The *New York Times* reports that in Japan, 'of last year's 10 best-selling novels, five were originally mobile phone novels, mostly love stories written in the short sentences characteristic of text-messaging' (Onishi 2008) with averages sales exceeding 400,000. The novels are not only read, but are commonly composed, on the phone: ' "It's not that they had a desire to write and that the cell phone happened to be there," said Chiaki Ishihara, an expert in Japanese literature at Waseda University who has studied mobile phone novels. 'Instead, in the course of exchanging [messages], this tool called the cell phone instilled in them a desire to write" ' (Norrie 2007). Nonetheless, the SMS novel largely conforms to the conventions of traditional literature, albeit in a new format. There is more potential for text-messaging as an artistic medium thanks to the underlying system for automated delivery. Instead of a dumb mechanism for periodically sending out a message, a system that responds to participants' input allows for a dynamic, nonlinear narrative structure.

Such a system can be described as a form of 'cybertext': '[In traditional literature] the performance of the reader takes place all in his head, while the user of cybertext also performs in an extranoematic sense' (Aarseth 1997, 1). Espen Aarseth draws the term from cybernetics, Norbert Weiner's study of dynamic systems involving a feedback loop (in this case between the text and its reader). In cybernetic terms, the text adjusts its output according to feedback from the reader. There is creative effort embodied in the physical action that feedback comprises. Further, the navigation of a cybertext involves the determination of a single textual experience from many possibilities:

> ... [it] is an object of verbal communication that is not simply one fixed sequence of letters, words, and sentences but one in which the words or sequence of words differ from reading to reading because of the shape, conventions, or mechanisms of the text. (Aarseth 1994, 51)

However, SMS is more complex than a platform for chatting, as the mobile phone is always situated in a particular physical environment. To consider the potential spatial dynamics of cybertext suggests a comparison to 'interactive fiction', a genre that emerged from the text-adventure

DOI: 10.1057/9781137469816.0012

games of the early 80s, in which an 'interactor' types out his actions in response to textual descriptions of a fictional world. The introduction to *Zork* (1979), the prototypical interactive-fiction work, has become a part of our cultural heritage: 'You are standing in an open field west of a white house with a boarded front door.' This author's memory of the scene is absolutely sensual: the peeling whitewash of the weary structure, the soft sound of high grass in the breeze—a mental construction that is at once foreboding and irresistible. *Zork*'s blunt prose writ in monochrome on an Apple IIe—being addressed directly, and in text, transports the reader/player intact into Zork's world. Should 'I' go inside the house? What will I find? To reveal one of countless narratives, at each step the reader/player must type commands such as 'Go north', 'Eat the food on the table', or 'Fight the grue'. Interactive fiction author Graham Nelson writes that,

> ...in an interactive medium, the beliefs and abilities of the protagonist are more than simply a painted backcloth, because the player participates in them. These special abilities might be called the 'magic' in the game's model world, in the broadest sense. (Nelson 2001, 379)

Calling on the reader to act as protagonist lends poetic power to interactive fiction. Furthermore, interactive fiction is explicitly spatial. Navigating a story is a matter of moving between 'rooms' and carrying 'objects' between them, terms which are not purely non-corporeal—a common practice when reading interactive fiction is to draw a map (with pencil and paper) to keep track of the narrative world. Consequently, to consider the mobile device as a cybertextual medium in this vein invites a direct confrontation between narrative space and the real world of the participant. Guy Debord, the primary provocateur of the Situationist International movement, recalled in 1955 that,

> A friend recently told me that he had just wandered through the Harz region of Germany while blindly following the directions of a map of London This sort of game is obviously only a mediocre beginning in comparison to the complete construction of architecture and urbanism that will someday be within the power of everyone. (Debord 1955)

The Situationists hoped to subvert the de facto modes of experiencing place imposed by the psychological conditions of society. Their theory of 'psychogeography', by Debord's definition, is 'the study of specific effects

DOI: 10.1057/9781137469816.0012

of the geographical environment, consciously organised or not, on the emotions and behaviour of individuals' (Debord 1955). Addressing the representation of space, it challenges the omnipotent perspective of the map, in which all features are reduced to categorical functions. Instead, psychogeography proposes the creation of alternative maps, which represent the unique possibilities and impressions that compose the transient realities of any place.

This appropriation and reimagining of on individual's environment resonates with other conceptual art paradigms that emerged in the 1960s—happenings, installations, and performance art. According to new media theorist Lev Manovich, these practices made art explicitly participatory in a way that prefigured the emergence of interactive computer art decades later (Manovich 2001, 56). Presciently, in 'Nontheatrical Performance' (1976), Allan Kaprow writes:

> My hunch about art is that a field that has changed in appearance as fast as it has must also have changed in meaning and function, perhaps to the extent that its role is qualitative (offering a way of perceiving things) rather than quantitative (producing physical objects or specific actions). (Kaprow 1993a, 177)

Many of the pieces by Kaprow and the Fluxus artists were instructions for 'nontheatrical performances'—they subverted traditional conventions by refusing to distinguish between performers and the audience. Kaprow's 'happenings', George Brecht's 'scores', and Yoko Ono's poems are all conceptual exercises that impose non-habitual constraints on the participant.

George Brecht's score is phrased in imperatives—it is not descriptive. Rather, it offers permission for the reader to perform (or imagine) the actions and draw her own conclusions. The frame of the artwork—as established by his prescription of an activity—makes use of what is available to the participant. Unlike the relative rigidity of cybertexts such as interactive fiction, Kaprow discusses 'a never-ending play of changing conditions between the relatively fixed or 'scored' parts of my work and the 'unexpected' or undetermined parts' (Kaprow 1993b, 11–12). Such investigations by the avant-garde explicitly elicited the emergent possibilities of social and spatial interaction in a way that anticipates the possibilities of text-messaging.

Elements of Fluxes scores are readily apparent in an SMS-based work created by Tim Etchells in 2001. Mistaken by many people for an advertising campaign, a series of flyers were distributed in London with the message 'Do you want to Surrender Control?' accompanied by instructions to send the message 'SURRENDER' to a phone number. The participant would then receive a series of text messages over a period of five days. As Etchells explains:

> *Surrender Control* is somewhere between a game and a set of dares. The instructions that people will receive vary enormously—some are orders to think about particular topics, others are invitations to look at the world in a particular way, other instructions are for actions, demands that people behave in particular ways or that they carry out particular tasks. (Locke 2003, n.p.)

As the experience progresses, the messages escalate in intensity, from thought experiments ('Remember last night'), to provocative actions ('Write the word SORRY on your hands. Leave it there until it fades'), to direct social engagement ('Dial a number different from that of a friend. If someone answers, try to keep them talking'). Etchells is primarily interested in the intimacy of the of medium:

> ... messages go direct to the phone of an individual, direct to a 'place' which is normally occupied by that person's friends, family or lovers. To create an art work for this context is an invitation, one could say, to whisper in the ears of strangers as they go about their daily business. Surrender Control tries to explore and push the boundaries of what is possible or even permissible in this context. (Locke 2003, n.p.)

Surrender Control is a seminal example of how powerful the minimal intervention of a text message can be. However, Etchell's framework purposefully does not allow participants to respond to the messages, preferring instead that they choose to act or not act in the reality of their lives. This is no way detracts from the piece, but it does not make full use of text-messaging's potential as cybertext. It is creative experience for the participants, but the frame does not adapt to their actions.

Knifeandfork's *The Wrench* (2007) attempts to synthesize some of the responsive strategies of chatbots and interactive fiction with conceptual concerns that echo those of the 20th century avant-garde. The piece recasts Primo Levi's 1978 novel, *The Monkey's Wrench*, as a text-message exchange between a participant and the protagonist, Tino Faussone, an itinerant steelworker. In Levi's original, Tino tells a series of stories that reflect a deeply contingent and physical relationship to the world. These themes, together with a quirky use of language

DOI: 10.1057/9781137469816.0012

and a first-person narrative, make Levi's character well-suited to the immediacy of text-messaging. In *The Wrench*, a modern-day Tino does not narrate his past experiences—rather, he engages the participant in a series of dialogues intended to convey the same themes as the book. These include everyday interventions where Tino needs help from the participant to navigate an unfamiliar city, asks participants to listen to the sounds of machines audible at that given moment, or waxes poetic about the nature of the labor that produced our impossibly intricate electronic devices.

As a result, *The Wrench* is not an SMS novel with predetermined messages. Instead, it employs an open-source software package developed by the artists, TXTML (http://txtml.org), to instantiate Tino as an artificially intelligent agent. Tino's dialogue is constructed in a way that is influenced by chatbots such as ELIZA—however, his progression through the space of potential narratives more closely mirrors the design of interactive fiction. Just as the player moves through the dungeons of Zork, charting one of many possible paths, in *The Wrench*, the participant, through responses over SMS, draws Tino into a particular series of conversations. In addition, Tino's messages draw on material dynamically generated from Internet content (via RSS feeds) which enables him to comment and respond to events in real time and in the real world, such as the weather or the outcome of last night's Yankees game. A flexible timing system is used so that Tino sends messages appropriate to the time of day, whether he is initiating the exchange or responding to a spontaneous message from the participant.

Like ELIZA, Tino is not necessarily meant to be convincingly human, but he is intended cultivate a human relationship with the participant. Unlike other SMS systems, the messages of *The Wrench* are in the voice of an identified character, Tino, and are sent from a standard phone number to which participants can send responses just as they would to ordinary friends. By asking participants about their own activities and philosophies, the piece inserts Levi's themes into the participant's everyday reality. For example:

TINO: just dropped off theresa, killing time. do you have much down time in your day?
PAUL: sometimes, depends if im working or not. im a freelancer.
TINO: me too, i like to be my own boss. i decide when to work and when to stop.
PAUL: damn right. that's the only way to go. (Knifeandfork)

DOI: 10.1057/9781137469816.0012

After opening a book or starting a movie, the fiction of the experience is contained within the bounds of the media. *The Wrench*, however, disrespects this barrier. In the words of a participant:

Tino forces me to reflect on my life and on life in general. His timing is unexpected, so in order to respond to him in a timely manner I have to interrupt the minutiae of my day and think about the questions he's asking. (Knifeandfork)

Inspired by *Surrender Control*, The Wrench is designed to take advantage of the fact that text-messaging as a medium is situated in the lives of its users. What happens beyond the interface of the phone is not extradiegetic, but the subject of the story itself.

Aarseth insists that the pleasure of cybertext is a result of executing the logic provided by the author in order to form a unique narrative:

In electronic narrative the procedural author is like a choreographer who supplies the rhythms, the context, and the set of steps that will be performed. The interactor, whether as navigator, protagonist, explorer, or builder, makes use of this repertoire of possible steps and rhythms to improvise a particular dance among the many, many possible dances the author has enabled...(Murray 1997, 152)

This is a clear example of Manovich's notion of how, with emerging media, the production of narrative has changed. With traditional storytelling,

... the database of choices from which narrative is constructed (the paradigm) is implicit; while the actual narrative (the syntagm) is explicit. New media reverse this relationship. Database (the paradigm) is given material existence, while narrative (the syntagm) is dematerialised. (Manovich 2001, 231)

But what does it mean for a cybertext to be experienced via a mobile device? Such a narrative specifies neither a syntagm nor a complete paradigm—though the possible texts of the messages might be constrained, the relationship of each message to the conditions of the real world in which it is received are not. Consequently, text-messaging blurs the boundary between a hermetic narrative space and the unpredictable logics of the real world. Employing strategies that echo nontheatrical performance, new forms of literature can therefore elicit the specific creativity of the human consciousness as it interacts with the environment, temporarily reorganizing how reality might be experienced.

Janet Murray writes, 'Participatory narrative ... raises several related problems: How can we enter the fictional world without disrupting it?

DOI: 10.1057/9781137469816.0012

How can we be sure that imaginary actions will not have real results?'
(Murray 1997, 103). With an SMS cybertext in the real world, we cannot.
There is actual physical danger in mobility, and there is no guarantee of a
hermetic space—the syntagm might extend beyond both the prefigured
narrative and the participants' habitual experience of the world. Yet it is
possible that by specifically framing everyday experience in a way that
invites the same creative agency exercised by the reader of cybertext, a
poetic transformation of the mundane may occur. As the Situationist
Raoul Vaneigm puts it:

> The laboratory of individual creativity transmutes the basest metals of
> daily life into gold through a revolutionary alchemy ... The new artists
> of the future, constructors of situations to be lived, will undoubtedly have
> immediacy as their most succinct—though also their most radical—demand.
> (Vaneigm 2001)

The subtle insistence of the text message and its imaginative potential
is a step in that subversive direction.

References

Aarseth, Espen. 1994. 'Nonlinearity and Literary Theory', in George
    P. Landow (ed.), *Hyper/Text/Theory* Baltimore: The John Hopkins
    University Press.

Aarseth, Espen. 1997. *Cybertext: Perspectives on Ergodic Literature.*
    Baltimore: The John Hopkins University Press.

Brecht, George. 1961. *Direction.*

Debord, Guy. 1955. 'Introduction to a Critique of Urban Geography',
    trans. Ken Knabb, *Les Lèvres Nues 6.*

Hillebrand, Friedhelm, ed. 2001. *GSM and UMTS: The Creation of Global
    Mobile Communication.* Hoboken: Wiley.

Kaprow, Allan. 1993a. 'Nontheatrical Performance', in *Essays on the
    Blurring of Art and Life.* Berkeley: University of California Press.

Kaprow Allan. 1993b. 'Notes on the creation of a Total Art', in *Essays on
    the Blurring of Art and Life.* Berkeley: University of California Press.

Knifeandfork. 2007. 'The Wrench'. http://knifeandfork.org/thewrench
    (accessed March 20, 2008).

Locke, Matt. 2003. 'Tim Etchells—Surrender Control'. *TEST,* July
    14. http://test.org.uk/2003/07/14/tim-etchells-surrender-control/
    (accessed August 11, 2014)

DOI: 10.1057/9781137469816.0012

Manovich, Lev. 2001. *The Language of New Media*. Cambridge: The MIT Press.

Murray, Janet. 1997. *Hamlet on the Holodeck*. Cambridge: The MIT Press.

Nelson, Graham. 2001. *The INFORM Designer's Manual*. St. Charles: The Interactive Fiction Library.

Norrie, Justin. 2007. 'In Japan, cellular storytelling is all the rage'. *The Sydney Morning Herald*, December 3.

Onishi, Norimitsu. 2008. 'Mobile phone novels ring up big sales, but critics fear for Japanese literature'. *New York Times*, January 23.

Sales, Leila. 2008. 'Lst ngt was...' *The Leila Texts*. http://theleilatexts. blogspot.com/2008/03/lst-ngt-was.html (accessed March 20, 2008).

Vaneigm, Raoul. 2001. *The Revolution of Everyday Life*, trans. Donald Nicholson-Smith. London: Rebel Press.

Vnunet. 2008. 'SMS Messaging Surges over the Holiday'. http://www. vnunet.com/vnunet/news/2206783/sms-messaging-surges-holiday (accessed March 20, 2008).

DOI: 10.1057/9781137469816.0012

Part III
Knowledge and Stories

Berry, Marsha and Max Schleser. *Mobile Media Making in an Age of Smartphones*. New York: Palgrave Macmillan, 2014. DOI: 10.1057/9781137469816.0013.

▶

DOI: 10.1057/9781137469816.0013

When assessing the significance of the mobile phone in everyday life, statistics offer a compelling argument. According to the UNFPA: United Nations Population Fund report in 2007, more people now live in cities than in rural areas and the medium that the majority of people have access to on a global scale is the mobile device. Marketwire reports that 'millions of people are now experiencing connectivity to the world for the first time through wireless and changing their economic, social and political fortunes forever (Livingston [online] 2008). In 2011, the International Telecommunications Union (ITU)—the United Nations specialized agency for information and communication technologies—estimated the number of mobile users world wide to be 5.9 billion, or 86.7% of the world population. This significantly outstrips the number of Internet users worldwide, which the ITU estimates to be 34.7% of the world population (*ITU* online). While not all mobile users have Internet capabilities, the mobile phone has become the primary means of inter-net access for many, being the sole means of internet access for 50% of African and Asian internet users (*On Device Research* online 2012).

Far from simply being an alternative means of connectivity to the PC, mobile media present the opportunity for new forms and formats of storytelling, knowledge dissemination, and new audience experiences. In his recent book *The Mobile Audience* (2012), Martin Rieser addresses the way that mobile media facilitate new relationships with and roles for audiences. These roles are not yet fully understood, and Rieser asks 'in what ways can the new modes of audience engagement and participation in dispersed or mobile interactive art works, be evaluated?' (Rieser, 2012, p 4). Rieser suggests that the mobile media are 'in pressing need of exploration, definition and documentation for the benefit of a wider audience' (Rieser 2012, 4). This section places the intersection of knowledge and storytelling in the context of three case-studies dealing with m-Agriculture, digital storytelling with a group of young Aboriginal people and creative writing practices.

The proliferation of digital and interactive media, including the web and mobile media, have given rise to a number of concepts and terms to describe our changing relationships with media. Whether described as 'remix culture' (Lessig 2008), 'participatory culture' (Jenkins 2009) or the more ambiguous 'Web 2.0', central to all is the ethos of a more participatory media experience. David Gauntlett summaries these concepts when describing as central to Web 2.0 'the idea that online sites and services become more powerful the more that they embrace [the] network of potential collaborators. Rather than just seeing the Internet as a broadcast channel, which brings an audience to a website (the '1.0' model), Web 2.0 invites users in to play' (Gauntlett 2012, 5). The role of the audience is no longer that of a passive receiver, but as Gauntlett suggests, one in which the audience is invited not only to play but also participate. The audience is recast as an active producer as well as consumer of media. This has led to concepts such as the 'produser' (Bruns 2008; Wintonick 2005), to account for the dual role of the audience as creators and consumers of media and expressing the more dynamic relationship with media.

Smartphones not only provide the opportunity to access a media production tool, but are also part of a media ecology providing access to the Internet. While exploring these prospects this section also takes a critical position discussing the 'participation gap' and technological determinism. The discussed mobile projects provide innovative solutions to intergenerational knowledge exchange, which acknowledges the centrality of Aboriginal Elders (and older community members) in transmitting and sustaining Aboriginal 'ways of knowing', creative writing and the dissemination of knowledge in small-scale farming communities in Africa.

References

Bruns, Axel. 2008. *Blogs, Wikipedia, Second Life, and Beyond: From Production to Produsage*. Bern: Peter Lang.

Gauntlett. David. 2010. *Making is Connecting: The Social Meaning of Creativity, from DIY and Knitting to YouTube and Web 2.0*. London: Polity Press.

International Telecommunications Union (ITU). www.itu.int/ITU-D/ict/statistics/at_glance/KeyTelecom.html (2012) [online].

Jenkins. Henry. 2009. *Confronting the Challenges of Participatory Culture*. Cambridge, Massachusetts. The MIT Press.

Lessig, Lawrence. 2008. *Remix: Making Art and Commerce—Thrive in the Hybrid Economy*. London: Penguin Press.

Livingstone, Sonja. 2008 [online] Mobile Connections Reach 4 Billion Worldwide—More Than 100 Operator Commitments to Next Generation Mobile Networks with LTE.http://www.marketwire.com/press-release/3G-Americas-932790.html (accessed December 26, 2008).

DOI: 10.1057/9781137469816.0013

On Device Research 2012 http://ondeviceresearch.com/blog/new-internet-audience-emerges-in--developing-countries (2012) [online]

Rieser, Martin (ed). 2011. *The Mobile Audience: Media Art and Mobile Technologies*. Amsterdam-New York: Rodopi.

UNFPA:United Nations Population Fund (2007) Urbanization: A Majority in Cities [online] http://www.unfpa.org/pds/urbanization. htm (accessed February 02, 2008).

Wintonick, Peter in Blassnigg, Martha (2005) Documentary Film at the Junction between Art, Politics, and New Technologies. Leonardo Reviews, 443 [online] http://www.leonardo.info/ reviews/mar2005/ doc_blassnigg.html (accessed December 12, 2005).

DOI: 10.1057/9781137469816.0013

8

Sauti ya Wakulima: Listening to the Voice of Tanzanian Farmers

Eugenio Tisselli

Abstract: *E-agriculture defines an emerging field in which information and communication technologies are applied to improve the dissemination of accessible, up-to-date information on agriculture, particularly in rural areas, and to increase food production, both in quantity and quality (WSIS, 2003). Mobile communication technologies are presently the main focus of e-agriculture. In Africa, where most of the development projects for agriculture are concentrated, Internet usage is still low, but more than a third part of the population in Africa are cellphone owners, and this rate is growing fast (International Telecommunications Union, 2010). Sauti ya wakulima, 'The voice of the farmers' in Swahili, is an e-agriculture project that directly addresses the social context of rural agriculture in Tanzania.*

Berry, Marsha and Max Schleser. *Mobile Media Making in an Age of Smartphones.* New York: Palgrave Macmillan, 2014. DOI: 10.1057/9781137469816.00014.

DOI: 10.1057/9781137469816.00014

In this chapter I explore how mobile technologies, when used in a culturally respectful way, may help us to rethink and enhance the dissemination of knowledge in small-scale farming communities. Learning approaches in the context of agriculture have called for media strategies that contribute to the enhancement of farmer participation and the strengthening of their traditional knowledge (Pimbert 2006). As a response to this call, I will present *Sauti ya wakulima*, a project that attempts to apply smartphones and web-based services to encourage the creation of networks of mutual learning in Tanzanian rural communities.

The lure of technology

The idea that technologies may solve the problems of humanity as if by magic is incredibly persistent. It stands even after those technologies have generated negative outcomes that exceed their benefits. Time and again, artifacts as diverse as telephones or tractors generate utopian hopes. *The basic conceit is always the same: new technology will bring universal wealth, enhanced freedom, revitalized politics, satisfying community, and personal fulfillment* (Winner 1997, 1001). This mindset is commonly known as *technological determinism*, a notion that regards technology as neutral since it does not alter the *natural* course of human evolution toward perfection, but merely shortens the path to it. Hence, technology becomes *naturalized* as well and, for this reason, technological determinism tends to deny the ideological values inscribed in it. However, more nuanced visions of technology tend to adopt a holistic perspective and acknowledge its malleability by clearly identifying the interplay of its design, the political negotiation regarding its modes of usage, and the social and environmental contexts in which it is used (Feenberg 1999).

Technologies such as telephones or tractors have not failed their utopian purposes completely. If anything, they have shown us that technologies tend to solve problems while creating new ones. Telephone, for example, made new ways of communication possible while transforming communication itself, by rendering it increasingly disembodied and distant. Telephones thus represent a paradox: that of a greater isolation as consequence of a greater ability to communicate. By unfolding this paradox, a limit to the expansion of technologies seems to appear,

DOI: 10.1057/9781137469816.00014

beyond which the artifacts we create start to defeat their purpose and turn against ourselves (Illich 2001).

One of the latest waves of technological determinism is closely related to information and communication technologies (ICTs). The integration of mobile networks and the Internet has come to symbolize the key to a contemporary utopia in which supposedly *flat*, decentralized and demo-cratic networks will replace hierarchical models of labor, learning, and leisure. And, interestingly enough, the mobile phone as a technological panacea is quickly entering the field of agriculture and displacing older inventions, such as tractors, which represent an outdated model of large-scale, centralized industrial growth.

Connected farmers

Smallholder farmers in Kenya are estimated to sell an average of 3 to 5 litres of cow milk per day; calculations show that 15 litres per day is the required production to bring a family over the poverty line. This state-ment, which identifies a concrete problem suffered by farmers in Kenya, is featured on the homepage of iCow (iCow: http://icow.co.ke retrieved November 15, 2013). iCow is an SMS-based mobile informa-tion service that aims to help smallholder farmers to increase milk production. Farmers who subscribe to this service receive SMS alerts about different issues related to the life cycle of their cows, such as optimizing their health and nutrition, managing their estrus cycle or calculating the costs of milk production. According to the iCow team, 42% of the farmers who remained loyal to the service reported increased incomes, and 56% of them attributed those profits to an increase in milk yield. iCow is one of the most popular initiatives in e-Agriculture, a field that has rapidly gained consistency and accept-ance in development circles.

e-Agriculture (also known as m-Agriculture) brings together different activities and initiatives in which ICTs, particularly mobile phones, are applied to the improvement of smallholder agriculture and rural liveli-hoods. Presently, e-Agriculture is largely concentrated in Africa, where 63% of the population owns a mobile phone according to ICT Facts and Figures. While this figure is still low compared to other regions of the world, Africa has the fastest-growing rate of mobile penetration. A survey conducted in Tanzanian farms offered an overview of how mobile

DOI: 10.1057/9781137469816.00014

phones were actually used in the agricultural activities carried out by farmers, and identified five potential areas of application:

1 Accessing timely information.
2 Making markets more efficient and transparent.
3 Providing advance warning of weather and other risks.
4 Accessing complementary services such as mobile banking.
5 Aiding in general communication and coordination.

(Furuholt and Matotay 2011)

The *ICT4AG* conference, which took place in November 2013 in Kigali, Rwanda, gathered many of the major actors of *e-Agriculture*. It was an enthusiastic meeting of policy-makers, ICT specialists, entrepreneurs, and representatives of development organizations from around the world, all of them galvanized by an environment, which celebrated the *transformative* power of ICTs. Their discourse concentrated on how to best harness and apply the benefits of ICTs to increase productivity, efficiency and income of small-scale farmers. *ICTs are driving a new revolution* was the overarching message, and it left very little room for critical questioning. Despite the noticeable absence of farmers' voices at the conference, compelling messages were delivered: *let's put farmers at the center of development, let's use ICTs to bring them to a new level.* Despite these good intentions, the *technological determinism* revealed by these slogans is, unfortunately, shortsighted, and may be potentially harmful for farmers in the long run.

The reductionist problem-solving stance characteristic of *technological determinism* may be detected in popular *e-Agriculture* initiatives such as *iCow, M-Farm* (http://mfarm.co.ke/) and many others. Evgeny Morozov defines this trend as *solutionism*: a normal problem-solving apparatus gone into overdrive (Morozov 2013). Thanks to ICTs, Morozov claims, new types of solutions that weren't possible a few years ago are now ready at hand. These solutions may prompt uncritical redefinitions of supposed problems that evade complex social, political, and environmental considerations in favor of a new, attractive infrastructure for problem-solving that sidesteps systemic reforms and degrades awareness. Morozov observes the rise of *solutionist* initiatives, which are being deployed simply because of the technically awesome perspectives they offer while ignoring the social and political implications that they might smuggle through the back door.

DOI: 10.1057/9781137469816.00014

In the context of agriculture, isolating specific problems and applying purely technical solutions to solve them has historically caused harm. If there is a lesson to be learned from the *Green Revolution* in agriculture of the 1960s and 1970s, it is that technological solutions that initially produced impressive crop yields created systemic changes which, in the long run, gave way to negative effects (Roberts 2008). Tractors, chemical fertilizers, and pesticides introduced in developing countries during the *Green Revolution* degraded the quality of arable land while prompting small-scale farmers into a spiraling dependency on expensive inputs.

Could the new mobile-driven agricultural revolution promote a new kind of dependency on electronic devices, energy, and connectivity? While some *e-Agriculture* initiatives may have brought short-term benefits to long-neglected smallholder farmers, it is necessary to think carefully whether those benefits will still hold over time. There is a real risk that *solutionism* in *e-Agriculture* may leapfrog learning of agricultural skills and knowledge by jumping to quick, short-term solutions. Information about cropping techniques, livestock keeping, and market prices are delivered to farmers via SMS messages. This information may be useful indeed, but are *e-Agriculture* entrepreneurs really listening to what the farmers value and need? Can *e-Agriculture* truly empower farmers, or will it leave them—literally—to their own devices? Learning approaches in agriculture have long criticized this sort of *solutionist* delivery of merely operative information, calling instead for truly participatory processes in which farmers may really become central, autonomous actors (Ashby 1990; Pimbert 2006).

Sauti ya wakulima

How can farmers be regarded not just as clients of information delivered through ICTs, but also as generators and disseminators of content? *Sauti ya wakulima, The voice of the farmers* in Swahili, is an *e-Agriculture* project (http://sautiyawakulima.net) that directly addresses the socio-agricultural context of rural farming in Tanzania and encourages farmers to share their knowledge. The project started in January 2011, after my colleagues Dr Angelika Hilbeck, Juanita Schlaepfer-Miller and myself conducted a series of interviews with farmers living in the area Bagamoyo. We initially interviewed these farmers with the purpose of

DOI: 10.1057/9781137469816.00014

learning about their practices, the challenges they were facing, and their strategies for coping with climate change and other related problems. We then invited the farmers to participate in the creation of an on-line, collaborative knowledge base about their observations of unprecedented climatic events, and to use smartphones as mobile reporting tools. We explained that the images and voice recordings captured with the smartphones would be directly uploaded to a shared and accessible website. Thus, farmers would become climate reporters, and their observations would be instantly visible to those who entered the website. Although the type of phones we offered the farmers was not available in Tanzania at that time, GSM phones were present in every farm and were intensely used: not just to communicate with other people, but also to connect with agricultural markets and to carry out monetary transactions through *e-Banking*. Moreover, despite the fact that none of the farmers had accessed the Internet before, they had all heard about it through their children. The farmers saw the potential of the project and thus accepted our invitation to participate, as they understood that it could become a useful platform for making their voices broadly heard.

Currently, the participants of *Sauti ya wakulima* are a group of five men and five women chosen by a larger community. They meet every week to share the two available smartphones we provided, and pass them on to others. Each participant has the task of using the smartphone to document relevant issues previously agreed upon, and upload these contents to the website. The contents generated by farmers are fragmented into *messages* formed by one picture, one voice recording that may explain what is shown in the picture, a corresponding set of geographical coordinates and a descriptive keyword or *tag*. An open source app called *ojoVoz* (http://ojovoz.net) was specifically developed to help farmers compose and post these messages easily.

The group is overseen by a local coordinator who schedules weekly meetings in which participants not only rotate the smartphones, but also review and discuss the latest messages uploaded to the website. On the website, the aggregated messages form a knowledge base that may be explored by date, geographical location, or by clicking on one of the descriptive tags that appear on a tag cloud. The aim of the website is to act as a reflexive interface where farmers can discuss and make sense of their contents. However, it also seeks to allow local extension officers to monitor and respond to the reports made by farmers, and scientific researchers to gain a direct insight of what is happening in the farms.

DOI: 10.1057/9781137469816.00014

Farmers quickly adopted *Sauti ya wakulima* and, after a few months, they started to claim ownership of the project by reshaping its goals and using the smartphones according to their own interests and aspirations. The participants followed the original goal of the project by documenting the direct and indirect effects of climate change, such as droughts, floods, pests, or crop diseases. However, they also used the smartphones as means to consult other fellow farmers on positive and negative aspects of farming and coping techniques, advertise good sources of input material and their own products, or even expand their social networks through dialogues and interviews. The farmers' transformation of the research goals may be considered as an indicator of their motivation to use the mobile devices to reflect and communicate their own values, opinions, and practices. This unexpected deviation from the original objective of the project does not necessarily mean that climate change is not an important issue for the participants, but rather suggests that the tools were perceived as unique means for creating an environment for mutual learning. Participants of *Sauti ya wakulima* understood that sharing knowledge about effective farming techniques and strengthening social bonds could become crucial factors when facing complex challenges, such as climate change (Figure 8.1).

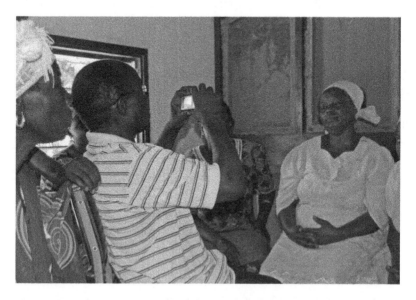

FIGURE 8.1   *Interviews using smartphones. Photo by Juanita Schlacpfer-Miller CC BY-BC-ND*

DOI: 10.1057/9781137469816.00014

What the farmers said about Sauti ya wakulima

An important lesson learned in *Sauti ya wakulima* is that true farmer-led research should ideally be open-ended, so that farmers may exercise their freedom to redefine and reshape its methodology and objectives. In the following paragraphs, some of the most revealing insights provided by the participants of *Sauti ya wakulima* are transcribed.

1.   How was the project useful for you?

—It helped us to become familiar with different kinds of agricultural problems.

—It allowed us to learn from each other, even from farmers who live far away.

—We were able to meet and learn from other farmers by interviewing them.

—The web page can improve our communication with the local extension officer.

—The project has brought cohesion to the group thanks to the meetings and discussions.

2.   What did you learn from the project?

—I learned how to properly plant maize thanks to a picture sent by a colleague.

—One picture helped us to identify a mango fungus.

—I received timely advice after posting pictures of a grasshopper pest.

—Computers are not just fancy things for rich people in towns: they can also be used by farmers to help them solve their problems.

3.   How can the project be improved?

—Very few farmers know about the Internet, so there is a need to provide more resources and training.

—By linking the project to a TV or radio show.

—Include people from different areas so we can learn from those who are far away, doing different things.

—We need to get feedback when we report a problem.

DOI: 10.1057/9781137469816.00014

Conclusions

The farmers in Bagamoyo transformed *Sauti ya wakulima* by leading the project toward goals and meanings that were consistent with their needs and aspirations. Through their act of resignifying tools and research objectives, they enriched the project with values that contrast with those usually found in many *e-Agriculture* projects. As a result, *Sauti ya wakulima* highlights the importance of sharing knowledge and carrying out truly participatory research instead of offering prepackaged, *solutionist* information services with short-term utilitarian purposes. Whereas the sheer excitement generated by the new possibilities offered by ICTs may be the starting point for many *e-Agriculture projects*, *Sauti ya wakulima* focuses instead on the importance of sharing *voice* as a form of solidarity and a vehicle for mutual learning.

Applying technological solutions to agriculture, or to any field of human activity for that matter, is a constant and mindful quest for equilibrium. It entails careful thinking about the varied and complex consequences of technologies in relation to the specific social and ecological contexts in which they are put to use. And just how much technology is enough before crossing the threshold that leads from benefits to damage?

The participants of *Sauti ya wakulima* also challenged the *official* notion of *expertise*, understood as a system of knowledge exercised exclusively by those who hold degrees and titles. By helping farmers to make their voices heard, the project unfolded a wealth of knowledge and creativity, revealing that Tanzanian farmers are already adapting to climate change in unexpected and effective ways. Our findings support those of scientific studies on adaptation to climate change, which claim that farmers are not only willing to learn from their own experience, but also to share it and learn from their neighbors (Abay, Gebregiorgis and Hailemichael 2012).

In *Sauti ya wakulima*, we have tried to encourage and strengthen reciprocal values by redefining how the smartphones are used and shared. Instead of delivering one smartphone to each farmer, only two of them were made available for a group of ten. This is not only a way to save resources but, more impsortantly, a way of transforming smartphones, considered to be essentially individual devices for *mass self-communication* (Castells 2009), into communal tools. We found that the shared usage of smartphones created a sense of compromise within the group: whenever it was somebody's turn to use a smartphone, that

DOI: 10.1057/9781137469816.00014

person felt the responsibility to document things that could be relevant and meaningful to all.

References

Abay, Fetien, Gebregiorgis, Gebrecherkos and Hailemichael, Lemlem. 2012. 'Farmer-led Documentation in Ethiopia', in L. Veldhuizen, A. Waters-Bayer, C. Wettasinha, W. Hiemstra (eds), *Farmer-led Documentation: Learning from Prolinnova Experiences* http://www. prolinnova.net/content/farmer-led-documentation-learning-prolinnova-experiences-1 (retrieved November 15, 2013).

Ashby, Jacqueline. 1990. 'Small Farmers' Participation in the Design of Technologies', in M. Altieri, S. Hecht (eds), *Agroecology and Small Farm Development*. Boca Raton: CRC Press.

Castells, Manuel., 2009. *Communication Power*. New York: Oxford University Press.

Feenberg, Andrew. 1999. *Questioning Technology*. New York: Routledge.

Furuholt, Bjorn, and Matotay, Edmund. 2011. 'The Developmental Contribution from Mobile Phones accross the Agricultural Value Chain in Rural Africa', *The Electronic Journal of Information Systems in Developing Countries* 48 (7): 1–16.

Illich, Ivan. 2001. *Tools for Conviviality*. London: Marion Boyars Publishers Ltd.

Morozov, Evgeny. 2013. *To Save Everything Click Here*. London: Allen Lane.

Pimbert, Michel. 2006. *Transforming Knowledge and Ways of Knowing for Food Sovereignty*. London: International Institute for Environment and Development.

Roberts, Wayne. 2008. *The No-Nonsense Guide to World Food*. Oxford: New Internationalist Publications.

Winner, Langdon. 1997. 'Technology Today: Utopia or Dystopia?' *Social Research* 64 (3): 989–1017.

DOI: 10.1057/9781137469816.00014

9

Digital Storytelling and Aboriginal Young People: An Exploration of Digital Technology to Support Contemporary Koori Culture

Fran Edmonds

▶

Abstract: *A digital 'participation gap' continues: not all media ecologies are created equal. Developing digital literacy and media skills are necessary for young Australian Aboriginal people to have equal opportunities for completing their education, to achieve productive online civic engagement (cyber citizenship), and to reap the benefits of the digital economy. This chapter discusses how digital stories (short films) were developed using images and information made on mobile devices and retrieved from individual's Facebook sites. How this information (photographs, videos, music, etc.) is created and shared via participants' digital stories is explored in relation to developing digital literacy skills that support Aboriginal youth culture.*

Berry, Marsha and Max Schleser. *Mobile Media Making in an Age of Smartphones.* New York: Palgrave Macmillan, 2014. DOI: 10.1057/9781137469816.0015.

DOI: 10.1057/9781137469816.0015

Aboriginal people from southeast Australia are referred to as Koori. In 2013 a pilot digital storytelling workshop was conducted with a group of young Aboriginal people associated with Bert Williams Aboriginal Youth Services (BWAYS) in an inner northern suburb in Melbourne, Victoria, Australia. The workshop was developed to better understand how Aboriginal young people are using digital technology in ways that support contemporary Aboriginal youth culture and identity. A focus group discussion with participants and consultants involved in the workshop, provided feedback that will contribute to the development of future digital storytelling projects. These new workshops will be conducted with other groups of Aboriginal young people and Elders as part of the 'Aboriginal young people in Victorian and Digital Storytelling' Australian Research Council Linkage Project from 2014 to 2017.

This chapter discusses the adoption of a collaborative participatory methodology, which included a whole-of-community approach to the research (Edmonds et al. 2014; Nakata 2007). All project contributors were recognized as knowledge or epistemic partners, providing their expertise to the project and contributing to its outcomes (cf. Marcus 2007). Ethnographic research methods were adopted, where the researcher worked with and learnt from the Aboriginal community (Madden 2010). This included working alongside young Aboriginal participants, older community members from BWAYS (and Elders) and two Aboriginal consultants: Yorta Yorta artist, Maree Clarke and Indigenous filmmaker and multimedia expert Kimba Thompson. The consultants also assisted the researcher in coordinating and facilitating the workshop.

Digital storytelling includes participants working with filmmakers, artists, and technology experts to produce personal short films/videos, while coming to terms with the technology. This supports a co-creative approach to media productions (cf. Burgess, Klaebe and McWilliam 2010). In this project the co-creative approach was expanded to include intergenerational knowledge exchange, which acknowledges the centrality of Aboriginal Elders (and older community members) in transmitting and sustaining Aboriginal 'ways of knowing' (cf. Martin 2003). Young people engaged with older members of the Aboriginal community to gain support and acquire additional cultural information for their stories, while elders were able to learn from youth's expertise in navigating the digital field, and to recognize the potential of digital technology for preserving and passing information on to future generations.

DOI: 10.1057/9781137469816.0015

Participants later discussed their digital storytelling experience as a process that provided new opportunities for disseminating information digitally, with the potential to broaden perspectives about Aboriginal histories across social and cultural boundaries.

Although many of the digital stories were difficult to tell, participants positioned their experiences within the context of resilience and as positive expressions of their Aboriginality. For some, their digital stories provided avenues for dealing with issues of fear and 'shame', revealing previously hidden histories connected with the continuing disruptive effects of colonization (Huebner 2013). Throughout Australian Aboriginal communities 'shame' is a concept with a broader understanding than the non-Aboriginal use of the word. It relates to imperatives connected with controlling and limiting information about circumstances or events that might embarrass the community in general. In this instance, digital stories were connected with the continuing impact of the stolen generations and the trauma and grief affecting the well-being of individuals, their families, and communities (cf. Edmonds et al. 2014).

Why do the project?

In this project, the role of intergenerational knowledge exchange is aligned with the understanding that for Aboriginal people storytelling is central to culture and learning (Yunkaporta 2007). While digital technology has transformed the way stories are transmitted, rapidly extending knowledge of Aboriginal people and their culture through expanding online social networks, stories also continue to embrace the integration of all aspects of life in accordance with Indigenous knowledge systems (worldviews) (Janke 2007). These worldviews are embedded in land and place and are expressed through narrative, art, song, performance, cultural and social practices, and contribute to understandings of connections to country and kinship networks (Nakata 2007).

The digital environment already provides Aboriginal youth and their communities with opportunities, often for the first time since colonization, to articulate and display their worldviews when and how they choose (Kral 2010). Additionally, the digital sphere engages large numbers of the Aboriginal population in Victoria, the majority of whom are under the age of 25 and who are regular users of mobile devices (DEECD 2010). Prolific use of these devices has fostered youth's expertise

DOI: 10.1057/9781137469816.0015

in creatively and interactively communicating through social networking sites such as Facebook, Instagram, and YouTube to form relationships and define their individual and social identities (Edmonds et al. 2012; Third et al. 2011). This active production and consumption of all kinds of information through digital media, has led some commentators to use the term 'produsers' to describe young people's online and other digital engagements (Collin et al. 2011).

Although Aboriginal young people demonstrate advanced digital literacy as 'produsers'—a result of the increasing accessibility of Web 2.0 enabled mobile devices—a 'participation gap' remains. This refers to limitations Aboriginal youth experience in acquiring appropriate education and training compared to their non-Indigenous peers. Thus, although Aboriginal young people are increasingly expert in managing digital technology for their own purposes, 'not all media ecologies are equal'. According to the American multimedia academic S. Craig Watkins, this means that without appropriate 'adult support, mentoring, or scaffolding of rich learning experiences', it is inevitable that these young people will continue to struggle to gain equal opportunities in the digital age (Watkins 2011).

Currently, little information about the use of digital technology by Aboriginal young people in southeast Australia is available. Most studies continue to focus on media production and the use of digital technologies by Aboriginal people from northern Australia (cf. Kral and Schwab 2012; Ormond-Parker et al. 2013). This constrains the potential to expand digital literacy skills in response to different Aboriginal communities. Without relevant information, which advances understandings of the specific cultural determinants of Aboriginal youth's access, control and communicative capacity via digital technology, this potentially reinforces homogenized views of Aboriginality throughout the country. In Victoria particularly, where colonization was rapid and widespread, and policies of assimilation were implemented earlier than elsewhere, Aboriginal people in southeast Australia continue to struggle to assert their culture in ways that are considered 'authentic' or 'real' (Peters-Little 2002). While some similarities exist between urban, regional, and remote Aboriginal Australia, binary representations of Aboriginal people via digital media, including representations of Aboriginal people in film and television as 'spatially divided between north and south, remote and urban, traditional and colonized' contributes to a misleading picture

DOI: 10.1057/9781137469816.0015

of Aboriginality and limits understandings of Aboriginal culture and history throughout the country (Davis and Moreton 2011). Such misunderstandings can contribute to Aboriginal people's experiences of racism, affecting mental health, social inclusion, and well-being (Ferdinand, Paradies, and Kelaher 2012).

In this project, digital storytelling as a research method, responds to and builds on the model adopted in the digital storytelling work by the Aboriginal filmmaker Kimba Thompson and the *Pitcha This* project, completed with six Victorian Aboriginal communities in 2007 (Thompson 2010). That project supports the contention that digital technology can assist in developing young people's creativity and build their identity, supporting a 'sense of community, belonging and connection', while advancing social inclusion on a scale previously unavailable in the nondigital world (YAW-CRC 2013). Additionally, for Aboriginal young people the production and sharing of digital content can contribute to understandings of who they are, their place in the community and their culture. These attributes can have a powerful impact on health and social outcomes for Aboriginal people, and are recognized as a key factor in building the resilience of Aboriginal youth (DEECD 2010).

How did we do the project?

Over 3.5 days six young people aged 15–23, and one older participant developed their stories, working with a range of technologies, including their own mobile phones, media pads, Apple Macintosh computers and laptops. They recorded their voiceovers using digital recording equipment and uploaded images and recordings to the Final Cut Pro editing suite.

Digital literacy and 'communities of practice'

To increase opportunities for informal intergenerational knowledge exchange and to assist youth's attendance, a culturally safe space for the participants was recommended by the manager from BWAYS. The workshop was conducted at the Aborigines Advancement League (AAL), a place of cultural and social significance for the Aboriginal community in Victoria and is accessed daily by Elders (NMA 2008). The importance of

DOI: 10.1057/9781137469816.0015

youth feeling secure in a familiar environment where they can 'explore Aboriginal culture and identity with Elders and community leaders' (ILNV 2010, 3), is recognized as essential for supporting Aboriginal young people, including in this instance their everyday experiences through the production of stories.

However, the AAL provided only limited access to the Internet and the Final Cut Pro editing suite, hence, the final day of the workshop was relocated to Kimba Thompson's film studio, Sista Girl productions. Nevertheless, the AAL provided a known space for participants to work in and supported informal knowledge exchange across the generations. This socially constructed, whole-of-community approach to learning aligns with the Swiss educational theorist, Etienne Wegner's idea of a 'community of practice'. Here 'situated learning' enables people to work together to create innovative solutions to difficult issues (Wegner 1998), and resonates with an Indigenous approach to community-based learning (Nakata 2007). Thus, youth and older members of the community were able to navigate the digital environment to witness and remember what has happened and what is currently happening in their lives and the lives of others (Iseke 2011).

Facebook: is it the new family photo album?

While young people revealed their potential to engage with technology and to elicit powerful first-hand narratives, some of the stories contained images that could potentially reinforce negative stereotypes, especially if viewers concentrated solely on the images at the expense of the narrative. Most participants downloaded images from their Facebook sites or retrieved them from their mobile phones.

Access to social network sites enables anybody with a smartphone to quickly create, store, and manage vast quantities of images. However, the proliferation of and instantaneous nature of images shared via mobile phones, including 'selfies', and pictures of 'big nights out', means that people now have an ever-increasing amount of imagery to draw on and to disseminate through their networks. Yet, few of these images are restricted or censored through the filter of the offline family photo album (see Vivienne and Burgess 2013). In this digital storytelling project, the retrieval of personal online images complicated the autobiographical approach, emphasizing youth's willingness

DOI: 10.1057/9781137469816.0015

to share material that they might regret posting in the digital sphere in later years.

This contrasts with earlier digital storytelling projects, before the prominence of Facebook and other online social media for storing and distributing images, as previously participants relied on taking photographs, using short films or making digital copies of images retrieved from personal family photo albums. For instance in the 2007 *Pitcha This* project, some of the participants relied on images from photographic archives, including the Koorie Heritage Trust's photographic collection, as well as images from their own family albums (Simondson 2011; Thompson 2010). In the Aboriginal community these older images provide personal, social, and political memories and are stored as treasured collections. These images are particularly relevant among a community where issues of identity and authenticity continue to be contested by mainstream audiences. Within the Aboriginal community many images are viewed as significant cultural reminders, affirming people's knowledge of who they are and where they come from (Huebner 2013). For the older participant in this project, Jenny, this system of obtaining the original hard copy of photographs from family and friends or other archival sources, has been updated to the digital realm, so that her images are now transferred to her iPad and stored as a personal digital photographic archive. While this enables her to share the images on Facebook, the archive itself remains the principle space for her retrieving, storing, and processing personal photographic information.

'Yarning' and digital storytelling: creating new oral histories

Working with the artists Maree Clarke and Kimba Thompson, the two Aboriginal consultants employed as facilitators during the workshop, provided a dynamic space for co-creativity to develop. Working from a community-based approach to digital storytelling, participants were able to learn from familiar and respected community experts to engage creatively in the storytelling process. The consultants also coordinated the Yarning Circle, where the oral traditions connected to storytelling were supported and later progressed to a digitized version. Yarning, in this instance, is an Indigenous convention for passing on information

DOI: 10.1057/9781137469816.0015

through relaxed and informal conversations, reflecting the oral traditions that are important for the transmission of knowledge among Aboriginal people (Bessarab and Ng'andu 2010).

The Yarning Circle included listening to Maree Clarke's story about her art practice, which alerted youth to the potential of exploring museum collections of their ancestors' art and material culture to inspire creative approaches for representing their histories and connections to place (Clarke and Edmonds 2013). While Maree's story provided an opportunity for participants to witness alternative approaches for developing their own autobiographical representations, most stories made during the workshop were restricted to the participant's recent past. However, the Yarning Circle did enable participants to reflect on their experiences and to share them among the group.

Once the stories were committed to text and read aloud in the recording studio, participants were concerned that their recordings did not adequately reflect a true representation of themselves. The participants commented that it would be preferable if their voiceovers sounded conversational, more akin to yarning. 'Yarning' was therefore reinforced as an important cultural signifier for presenting and retaining stories in the digital realm. As the young participants below acknowledge:

> [In the recording booth] I started just breaking [my text] up and putting it in [smaller] stories... I was trying to read it and put a little extra in it [make it] sound a bit more... like I was having a conversation...

Having a 'yarn'

In the Aboriginal community, digital stories are viewed as the new oral histories, enabling families and individuals to recollect and to reclaim their histories through images and words (Edmonds et al. 2014). The effect of transferring Indigenous histories and knowledge through cyberspace, has become a medium for speaking about and for telling and retelling stories that can now extend across large geographical boundaries, enabling vast networks of people to interact and to connect with stories of the past as remembered in the present. This has also been commented on by Indigenous scholars, who agree that the creation of digital narratives through word and image, and people's capacity for control over self-representation is providing powerful ways for Indigenous people to 'subvert the colonizer's indoctrination and champion indigenous expression in the political landscape' (Hopkins 2006, 343).

DOI: 10.1057/9781137469816.0015

Conclusion

Although the workshop presented some cautionary tales regarding the limitations of retrieving images from social network sites and reproducing them in autobiographical digital stories, overall this pilot project highlighted the significance of adopting a collaborative, community-based approach to digital storytelling. Aboriginal organizations, Aboriginal experts, and the participants themselves were integral for developing and supporting contemporary stories of Aboriginality in the digital age. The creative capacity of digital technology was acknowledged for its potential to increase digital literacy and new media skills, which promote the diversity of southeast Aboriginal culture, while an intergenerational approach to digital storytelling fostered Indigenous 'ways of knowing', highlighting the agentive capacity of digital technology to provide Aboriginal youth with the ability to explore and express representations of themselves, advancing knowledge of who they are and their place in the world.

References

Bessarab, Dawn and Bridget Ng'andu. 2010. 'Yarning about Yarning as a Legitimate Method in Indigenous Research', *International Journal of Critical Indigenous Studies* 3 (1): 37–50.

Burgess, Jean, Helen Klaebe and Kelly McWilliam. 2010. 'Mediatisation and Institutions of Public Memory: Digital Storytelling and the Apology', *Australian Historical Studies* 41: 149–165.

Clarke, Maree and Fran Edmonds. 2013. *Contesting the past: The survival of southeast Australian Aboriginal art in the 21st Century in Journeys* in South-South Cultural Relations, Mapping South online publication, The South Project online publication http://mappingsouth.net/edmonds-clarke/

Collin, Phillipa, Kitty Rahilly, Ingrid Richardson, and Amanda Third. 2011. *The Benefits of Social Networking Services: A Literature Review.* Melbourne: CRC for Young People, Technology and Wellbeing.

Davis, Therese and Romaine Moreton. 2011. '"Working in Communities, Connecting with Culture": Reflecting on U-matic to YouTube a National Symposium Celebrating Three Decades of Australian Indigenous Community Filmmaking', *Screening the Past* (31) http://www.screeningthepast.com/2011/08/%E2%80%9Cworking-in-

DOI: 10.1057/9781137469816.0015

communities-connecting-with-culture%E2%80%9D-reflecting-on-u-matic-to-youtube-a-national-symposium-celebrating-three-decades-of-australian-indigenous-community-filmmaking-2/ (accessed June 1 2014).

DEECD, Department of Education and Early Childhood Development (Vic), 2010. *The State of Victoria's Children 2009*. Melbourne, Victoria.

Edmonds, Fran, Christel Rachinger, Jenny Waycott, Philip Morrissey, Odette Kelada and Rachel Nordlinger. 2012. *'Keeping Intouchable': A Community Report on the Use of Mobile Phones and Social Networking by Young Aboriginal People in Victoria*. Melbourne: IBES, University of Melbourne.

Edmonds, Fran, Richard Chenhall, Michael Arnold, Tania Lewis and Susan Lowish. 2014. *Telling our Stories: Aboriginal Young People in Victoria and Digital Storytelling*. IBES, The University of Melbourne: IBES, The University of Melbourne.

Ferdinand, A., Y. Paradies, and M. Kelaher. 2012. *Mental Health Impacts of Racial Discrimination in Victorian Aboriginal Communities: The Localities Embracing and Accepting Diversity (LEAD) Experiences of Racism Survey*. Melbourne: The Lowitja Institute.

Hopkins, Candice. 2006. 'Making Things Our Own: The Indigenous Aesthetic in Digital Storytelling', *Leonardo* 39 (4): 341–344.

Huebner, Sharon. 2013. 'A Digital Community Project for the Recuperation, Activation and Emergence of Victorian Koorie Knowledge, Culture and Identity', in L. Ormond-Parker, A. Corn, C. Fforde, K. Obata and S. O'Sullivan (eds), *Information Technology and Indigenous Communities*. AIATSIS: 171–184.

ILNV, The Indigenous Leadership Network Victoria. 2010. Community Conversations. Melbourne.

Iseke, Judy M. 2011. 'Indigenous Digital Storytelling in Video: Witnessing with Alma Desjarlais', *Equity & Excellence in Education* 44 (3): 311–329.

Janke, Terri, ed. 2007. 'Managing Indigenous Knowledge and Indigenous Cultural and Intellectual Property', in M. Nakata and M. Langton (eds), *Australian Indigenous Knowledge and Libraries*. Sydney: UTSePress.

Kral, Inge. 2010. 'Generational Change, Learning and Remote Australian Indigenous Youth', *Centre for Aboriginal Economic Policy Research (CAEPR) Working Paper* 68/2010.

DOI: 10.1057/9781137469816.0015

Kral, Inge and Robert G. Schwab. 2012. *Learning Spaces: Youth, Literacy and New Media in Remote Indigenous Australia*. Edited by Centre for Aboriginal Economic Policy Research, Research School of Social Sciences, College of Arts and Social Sciences and The Australian National University: Australian National University. E Press.

Madden, Raymond. 2010. *Being Ethnographic: A Guide to the Theory and Practice of Ethnography/Raymond Madden*. London: Sage.

Marcus, George E. 2007. 'Collaborative Imaginaries', *Taiwan Journal of Anthropology* 5 (7): 1–17.

Martin, Karen (Booran Mirraboopa). 2003. 'Ways of Knowing, Ways of Being and Ways of Doing: Developing a Theoretical Framework and Methods for Indigenous Re-search and Indigenist Research', in K. McWilliams, P. Stephenson and G. Thompson (eds), *'Voicing Dissent': Journal of Australian Studies*. St Lucia, University of Queensland Press, 203–257.

Nakata, Martin. 2007. 'The Cultural Interface', *The Australian Journal of Indigenous Education* 36 (Supplement): 7–14.

NMA, National Museum of Australia. 2008. 'Collaborating for Indigenous Rights: Victorian Aborigines Advancement League', *Canberra*. http://indigenousrights.net.au/organisation.asp?oID=14 (accessed December 10, 2013).

Ormond-Parker, Lyndon, Aaron Corn, Cressida Fforde, Kazuko Obata and Sandy O'Sullivan, eds. 2013. *Information Technology and Indigenous Communities*. AIATSIS.

Peters-Little, Frances. 2002. '"Yet Another End Of An Aboriginal Film-Maker's Journey": A Personal Account of Aboriginal Documentary Filmmaking in the ABC', *Hecate* 28 (1): 42.

Simondson, Helen. 2011. 'Victorian Indigenous Communities and Digital Storytelling', *Screening the Past* (31). http://www.screeningthepast.com/2011/08/victorian-indigenous-communities-and-digital-storytelling/

Third, Amanda, Ingrid Richardson, Phillipa Collin, Kitty Rahilly and Natalie Bolzan. 2011. *Intergenerational Attitudes towards Social Networking and Cybersafety: A Living Lab*. Melbourne: CRC for Young People, Technology and Wellbeing.

Thompson, Kimba. 2010. 'Pitcha This - Indigenous Deep Listening Project'. http://www.youtube.com/watch?v=csy1FdjOu8M. (accessed November 10, 2013).

DOI: 10.1057/9781137469816.0015

Vivienne, Sonja and Jean Burgess. 2013. 'The Remediation of the Personal Photograph and the Politics of Self-representation in Digital Storytelling', *Journal of Material Culture* 18 (3): 279–298.

Watkins, S. Craig. 2011. 'Mobile Phones, Digital Media, and America's Learning Divide', http://dmlcentral.net/blog/s-craig-watkins/mobile-phones-digital-media-and-america%E2%80%99s-learning-divide (accessed May 30, 2011).

Wegner, Etienne. 1998. *Communities of Practice: Learning, Meaning, and Identity*. Cambridge: Cambridge University Press.

YAW-CRC, Young and Well Cooperative Research Centre. 2013. 'Connected and Creative'. http://www.yawcrc.org.au/connected-and-creative/engaging-creativity (accessed October 5, 2013).

Yunkaporta, Tyson. 2007. 'Aboriginal Pedagogies at the Cultural Interface', in *Draft Report for DET on Indigenous Research Project in Western NSW Region Schools, 2007–2009:* Department of Education and Training, NSW.

DOI: 10.1057/9781137469816.0015

10

Smartphone Screenwriting: Creativity, Technology, and Screenplays-on-the-Go

Craig Batty

Abstract: *From the typewriter to the computer, with good old pen and paper in between, screenwriters have experienced a shift in how they physically write their screenplays. Along with this shift has come a plethora of free and paid-for software packages to help with writing a screenplay, such as Final Draft, Celtx, and ScriptSmart. The idea of 'I'll have to write it all again' has changed to an idea of 'I can erase, re-write and copy and paste in seconds', and even the formatting take care of itself. Screenwriters today are thus able to spend more time writing and less time typing. The market now is awash with apps for screenwriters, from Scrivener to Slugline to Plotbot to StorySkeleton, and although they do not teach the craft of screenwriting per se, they do provide users with some of the tools needed to plan and write a screenplay.*

Berry, Marsha and Max Schleser. *Mobile Media Making in an Age of Smartphones.* New York: Palgrave Macmillan, 2014. DOI: 10.1057/9781137469816.0016.

DOI: 10.1057/9781137469816.0016

In the 1990 film *Misery*, writer Paul Sheldon is taken in by 'number one fan' Annie Wilkes to recover from a car accident, only to learn that she is a crazed maniac. Annie knows that Paul has just finished his manuscript for the last installment of the *Misery* series, and is dying to read it. When she does read it, she is disgusted by the foul language and at protagonist Misery's demise. She demands that Paul re-write the book under her editorial guidance, and because he needs help with his recovery, Paul has no choice but to do as she says.

Throughout the film Paul is locked in his bedroom, frantically trying to write the new novel. Confined to a wheelchair, he is literally trapped in Annie's house and metaphorically trapped in a nightmare situation. He is also trapped in his use of the second-hand typewriter bought for him by Annie, which has the letter 'n' missing. The typewriter becomes a symbolic object with its own narrative journey: from being forced upon Paul to being used by Paul, and eventually appropriated by Paul to re-gain his strength and attack Annie (see Batty and Waldeback, 2008, 52–53).

I want to suggest that the film's use of the typewriter is a symbol for the changes in technology taking place at the time; more specifically, that it represents the significant shift in how writing takes place. As I will explore, *Misery* represents a point in history when the shackles of writing practice were coming undone. Almost 25 years later and no longer tied to the typewriter, we write with smartphones and tablets anywhere and at any time, a plethora of digital tools and apps available to us. For screen-writing practice and the future of screen stories, especially in relation to mobile filmmaking, this potential needs to be explored. As Tolstoy said on the emergence of filmmaking:

> You will see that this little clicking contraption with the revolving handle will make a revolution in our life—in the life of writers. It is a direct attack on the old methods of literary art. We shall have to adapt ourselves to the shadowy screen and to the cold machine. A new form of writing will be necessary. (cited by Price, 2010, 24)

We might re-consider this in light of technology available to the screenwriter today. Although in most cases a screenplay is still written, the possibilities of how and where it is written are endless. Field writes that 'Typing should never get in the way of writing', and suggests that with the personal computer, 100 percent of a screenwriter's time can be spent writing as opposed to 25 percent with a typewriter, which required

DOI: 10.1057/9781137469816.0016

constant re-typing (1994, 219). With digital tools and apps we might say the same, where the ease of using a smartphone or tablet makes writing possible anywhere, any time, in the moment. Story ideas, character observations and snatches of dialogue can be recorded immediately, and via mobile media can within seconds be migrated, synthesized, or downloaded to screenwriting software, which can then be referred back to during the writing of the screenplay. Narratives can thus be developed and written on devices free from spatial and temporal constraints: screenwriting-on-the-go.

From typing to writing

First published in 1979, Syd Field's *Screenplay: The Foundations of Screenwriting* saw its third edition published in 1994, sold with the tagline, 'Includes a new chapter on screenwriting and computers'. The chapter is short at 12 pages, but nevertheless gives the screenwriter-at-the-time something to consider; and for the screenwriter today who could not work without technology, a stark reminder of how things were before the digital revolution.

Being confronted with a new writing instrument himself, Field writes: 'I thought that if I changed the way I wrote, it would somehow inhibit the creative process' (1994, 219). This positions creativity alongside writing; or more accurately, creativity alongside typing. Although a discussion of creativity and screenwriting is beyond the scope of this chapter (Waldeback and Batty 2012), we can suggest it as typically beginning long before any typing takes place, such as in story conceptualization, character development, and plotting. Nevertheless this was a concern for Field, who saw new writing instruments as scientific rather than artistic endeavors; an idea I will return to later.

As computers evolved, so did screenplay software programs. Field lists some of the early 'add-on' formatting tools to existing packages such as Microsoft Word and Final Draft: Scriptware, Warren Script Applications, Script Perfection, and SuperScript Pro (1994, 224–226). In the early 2000s, the BBC even developed its own formatting tool, Script Smart. With the exception of Scriptware and Warren Script Applications, these tools used adjectives to describe both the screenplay and the screenwriter, promising more than its functionality. 'Perfection', 'super', 'pro', and 'smart' mark the programs as not only enabling writing,

DOI: 10.1057/9781137469816.0016

but also making the writing the good. Using advertising language to mythologize the product (see Batty and Cain 2010, 151–184), the names allude to screenplays that will succeed. More recent apps such as Scrivener, Slugline, Plotbot, and StorySkeleton are not so alluring. Along with screenplay formatting software, technology has capitalized on the value of tools that help writers develop their screenplays so they can take an idea through various iterations and the screenplay many drafts. During script development, areas of work include identifying themes, strengthening characters, sharpening story structure, and polishing dialogue.

In this way, creative process is recognized as something that can be enhanced by digital intervention, connecting technology closely with creativity—and arguably, pedagogy. Asking the question, 'What about a program that inspires the screenwriter with ideas and story guidance?' Field (1994, 225) had little idea of the avalanche of digital screenwriting tools to come. At the time of writing some digital tools did exist, such as IdeaFisher, Plots Unlimited, Collaborator, and Corkboard. Collaborator was a basic tool that posed a series of simple questions to help build characters and structure, and was aimed at all writers, not just screenwriters. Corkboard, which worked with Final Draft, incorporated a system of plotting scenes on index cards that the writer could shuffle around until they were happy that the structure would hold the screenplay together (Field 1994, 226). Ironically, the index card system is something Field became well known for championing.

Millard is skeptical of some contemporary digital tools and apps. Referring to Final Draft and Dramatica in particular, both of which feature interactive development tools, she writes: 'Ironically, just as digital technologies and networked media are opening up new methods of sketching screen ideas and collaborating with others, much of the scriptwriting software may be serving to restrict the range of possible storytelling strategies on offer'. For example, 'Story templates from the likes of Syd Field, Christopher Vogler, and Robert McKee have migrated across to digital platforms' (Millard 2010, 21). Although questioning why such story templates are used is valid, we need to understand the context of what they are trying to achieve. Arguably, tools and apps that include structural templates and character-building exercises are aimed at novices predominantly. They are not necessarily spaces for seasoned professionals to experiment with an art/craft they are already confident in.

DOI: 10.1057/9781137469816.0016

Screenplays-on-the-go

Describing the development of computers for mass consumption, and specifically the need for an easy-to-use system of files, icons, and user paths, Ganz writes: 'Interface design was no longer dealing with ergonomics but with metaphors' (2011, 129). The index card system underlying Corkboard, which has recently been updated for the iPad and re-named 'Index Card', is a good example of this. With a series of 'cards' that can be shuffled around the screen, the user works with an interface that metaphorically represents the creative process undertaken by many screenwriters over many decades. As with Courier with its fixed pitch font 12-point font was retained in the move to computers because of its low memory requirement and still the industry standard for writing screenplays (see Trottier 2010), the fact that there is still a market for the index card system suggests that there exists a nostalgia for using traditional plotting techniques, where the sensory act of moving icons around on a screen with a finger is not dissimilar to the physical act of picking up and moving cards around on a desk or a wall.

A similar thing might be said for Scrivener, marketed through an endorsement by best-selling novelist Michael Marsha Smith on the apps iTune store as 'The biggest software advance for writers since the word processor' and which has functions to aid writers of all types (screenwriters, novelists, journalists, lawyers, academics). The purpose of this app is to allow users the freedom to create a piece of writing when and how they feel, from simple text composition to hyperlink importing, index card notation, and image embedding. For screenwriters using Scrivener, a comparison can be made to character scribbles, dialogue snatches, setting/world image banking and music being played to help with writing rhythm, all of which might have taken place alongside the typing of a screenplay. This is not to say that screenwriters no longer perform these tasks; rather, that an app like Scrivener can contain all such physical activities in one virtual space. Furthermore, as with using index cards to find the most effective order of scenes to tell the story, Scrivener is also able to temporarily 'bind' all elements of the writing/creating together to gauge how well things are working; to see whether the project is hanging together or not.

Maras notes that technological advances in development tools have led to conception and execution becoming less separated, meaning screenwriting is no longer a words-based activity but one open to other

DOI: 10.1057/9781137469816.0016

forms of creative development (2009, 180). Price agrees, arguing that 'the monolithic conception of the screenplay [...] is being overturned by cheap and readily available methods of production and distribution, returning film-making and screenwriting to the cottage industries they were at the beginning of cinema' (2014, 229).

Writing about phases of development, Maras argues that 'Digital technology can assist in reconnecting conception and execution, of introducing more acts of conceptualization alongside the execution' (2009, 185). Like much literature on screenwriting in the digital era, with its focuses on experimental, nonmainstream script development that privileges the writer-director, it is not clear whether Maras is referring to the execution of a screenplay (writing) or the execution of a film derived from a screenplay (production). However, since Maras's work focuses predominantly on the screenplay as a text in and of itself, we can assume that he means a screenplay. Thus, by reconnecting conception and execution the screenwriter can use computers, tablets, and smartphones in new and creative ways that both challenge and expand creative practices.

As an example, added functionalities in formatting programs such as Final Draft and Celtx enable screenwriters to use images, videos, text, sounds, and hyperlinks from their personal files and the Internet and weave them into their screenplay-in-progress to help with aspects such as factual research, character, and world visualization, and mood and tone building. In a similar way that the Simulcam allows directors to combine green screen simulations with their film-in-progress to see how it might eventually look (see Price 2014, 229), this kind of multitextual, interactive screenwriting practice speaks to the idea of 'scripting beyond the blueprint' (Maras 2009, 124–129). Screenwriters are literally and metaphorically freed from the constraints of formatting, able to annotate, improvise, and experiment with their work in ways that harnesses new and evolving creative practices.

As Talvio reminds us, 'The text of a screenplay on paper [or screen] is always only a partial record of the screen idea' (2014, 91). Therefore, the digital paratexts that evolve from these functions potentially achieve more than might be possible on the page. That said, from the perspective of the non-writer-director, we must consider that such tools are designed to aide screenwriters' craft skills and abilities to tell stories that others in the development and/or production pipeline will want to support/make. They are not, as Millard has called for, ways of combining pre- and post-production material into the screenplay (2010).

DOI: 10.1057/9781137469816.0016

Analytics, clouds and tweets

Scenepad is an app that allows users to write, develop, analyze, and collaborate on screenplays. It includes a function allowing multimedia from Tumblr accounts to be transferred into the work-in-progress. Developed by Stewart McKie, a British PhD candidate whose work focuses on 'proposing more social and analytic capabilities in screenwriting technology […] from a position informed by [his] day job as a business analyst and enterprise software selection consultant' (McKie 2014), the app is designed to provide factual information and collaborative tools to aide the development of a screenplay, namely through the writing and weaving together of individual scenes. Through its embracing of 'screenwriting 2.0' (McKie 2014), the app can visualize a screenplay in ways such as providing its most commonly used locations, words, and phrases, and providing the number of scenes in which particular characters appear. Users can annotate their screenplays with this information, and through Tumblr data such as photographs, create storyboards and moodboards for the scenes they are writing. Users can also collaborate on the writing of scenes, through multiple author/owner capabilities.

Scenepad also hosts external links of potential interest to screenwriters. For example, one is to the 'slow journalism' magazine Delayed Gratification, which has a regularly updated Infographics section. In a recent post named 'How to Win an Oscar', an analysis of the characters played by Best Actor and Best Actress winners in films released between 1928 and 2012 reveals the best way to win one of the prestigious awards is to write a screenplay about a North American fictional character, ideally from the present day or recent past, who works as a solider/lawman or performer, whom the audience never sees participating in sexual scenes, and who in the end does not die—at least on screen. Infographics such as this might be created predominantly for reader humour, but we cannot deny the ability technology has to capture, analyze, and visualize statistics in this way, freely accessible to the public and in this case, screenwriters. That this information is accessible via a link to a quite different source avows the potential importance that digital tools and apps such as Scenepad play for today's creative practitioners.

ScriptCloud, a simple app launched by McKie in 2007, searches for the most commonly used words in a screenplay and visualizes them in a similar way to the Jonathan Feinberg/IBM Corporation program Wordle. ScriptCloud was intended to test out the technological possibilities that

DOI: 10.1057/9781137469816.0016

might be afforded to the screenwriter, providing benefits that at the time may have not been imaginable (McKie 2014). Users of ScriptCloud can upload screenplays as text files into a private online library, where they can manage multiple script instances and generate multiple user-defined scriptclouds from the content; and they can also view scriptclouds generated from existing (produced) screenplays (McKie 2007, 222–223). There may be benefit to screenwriters in having this information available, such as being able to identify key words that reinforce the themes of the screenplay and identifying under- or over-use of particular verbs in screen directions, but from the perspective of digital/mobile script development tools this app is perhaps more about supplying information that might be useful than it is actively trying to shape creative practice.

In 2013 McKie developed Scenetweet, an app intended to help writers develop screenplays in 'snippets', constructing scenes as-they-go without the need to sit in front of a computer. Users can also comment on each other's work, providing immediate and cyclical feedback. Based on the Twitter format of no more than 140 characters at a time, Scenetweet is described on its landing page as 'the rebellious sibling of Scenepad' and is branded tonally as such. The following three reasons for using the app are given:

> I Live to Tweet:
> Good News—there is a cure!
> Just try writing a 120-page movie script, one tweet at a time.
> You'll be back to > 140 chars in a jiffy.

> Its a Friday Night!
> Write—even when wasted.
> I know. You've had a skinful of cider and a vindaloo or maybe two.
> But you can still crack off a Scenetweet right?

> Final Draft RIP
> Industry leader blah,blah,blah.
> Live dangerously. Try something else. Never did like drafts anyway.
> Free yourself from formatting. Release your chabungas!

As McKie told me, on the face of it the app appears jokey; yet I suggest that it actually achieves a great deal in encouraging writers to write and collaborate with others, more perhaps than McKie's other apps. One of the difficulties when writing a screenplay is to get started in the first place, and then maintain the momentum to complete a full draft. By offering screenwriters the opportunity to write in short installments, on-the-go, Scenetweet is perhaps less daunting than the other tools and

DOI: 10.1057/9781137469816.0016

apps described, especially for the beginner screenwriter. With its ability to generate content and develop the screenwriter's practice, Scenetweet may be marketed as a rebellious sibling to Scenepad and ScriptCloud but I would argue is more productive.

Conclusion

Many screenwriting tools and apps exist but they vary widely in what they offer screenwriting practice. Some are concerned with creating a space to write; some focus on screenplay layout and structure; and some embrace creativity and develop the screenwriter's practice. As such, the tools and apps surveyed do not share a common desire, such as to change screenwriting practice, but rather respond to market needs and technological possibilities. As Field reminds us, 'Screenwriting software will help you write it, but it won't tell you *what* to write, or *how* to write it' (1994, 229). There have been major technological developments since the time of Field's writing, and digital tools and apps do aim to provide more *what* and *how*. Nevertheless, every tool and app is still reliant on what the screenwriter brings to it. So whereas some tools and apps provide loose frameworks within which existing practice can happen and others offer mere gimmicks, there is and always will be a great deal to be said about the screenwriter's existing knowledge and methods of creative practice.

References

Batty, Craig. 2014. 'Introduction', in C. Batty (ed.), *Screenwriters and Screenwriting: Putting Practice into Context*. Basingstoke: Palgrave Macmillan, 1–7.

Batty, Craig and Waldeback, Zara. 2008. *Writing for the Screen: Creative and Critical Approaches*. Basingstoke: Palgrave Macmillan.

Celtx, computer software, available at https://www.celtx.com/index.html (accessed December 5, 2013).

Corley, E. L. and Miguel, J. 2014. 'White Space: An Approach to the Practice of Screenwriting as Poetry', in C. Batty (ed.), *Screenwriters and Screenwriting: Putting Practice into Context*. Basingstoke: Palgrave Macmillan, 11–29.

DOI: 10.1057/9781137469816.0016

Dramatica, computer software, available at http://dramatica.com (accessed December 5, 2013).

Field, Syd. 1994. *Screenplay: The Foundations of Screenwriting*, 3rd edn. New York: Dell Publishing.

Final Draft, computer software, available at https://www.finaldraft.com (accessed December 5, 2013).

Ganz, A. 2011. 'Let the Audience Add Up Two Plus Two. They'll Love You Forever: The Screenplay as a Self-Teaching System', in J. Nelmes (ed.), *Analysing the Screenplay*. Abingdon: Routledge.

Maras, Steven. 2009. *Screenwriting: History, Theory and Practice*. London: Wallflower Press.

McKie, Stewart. 2007. 'Scriptcloud.com: Content Clouds for Screenplays', in *Semantic Media Adaptation and Personalization, Second International Workshop* 221–224), IEEE.

McKie, Stewart. 2014. Personal communication, Monday March 10, e-mail.

Millard, Katherine. 2010. 'After the Typewriter: The Screenplay in a Digital Era', *Journal of Screenwriting* 1 (1): 11–25.

Millard, Katherine. 2011. 'The Screenplay as Prototype', in J. Nelmes (ed.), *Analysing the Screenplay*, 142–157. Abingdon: Routledge.

Plotbot, computer software, available at http://www.plotbot.com (accessed December 5, 2013).

Price, Steven. 2010. *The Screenplay: Authorship, Theory and Criticism*. Basingstoke: Palgrave Macmillan.

Price, Steven. 2014. *A History of the Screenplay*. Basingstoke: Palgrave Macmillan.

ScenePad, computer software, available at http://www.tripos.biz (accessed December 5, 2013).

Scenetweet, computer software, available at http://scenetweet.com (accessed December 5, 2013).

ScriptCloud, computer software, available at http://scriptcloud.tripos. biz (accessed December 5, 2013).

Scrivener, computer software, available at http://www.literatureandlatte. com/scrivener.php (accessed December 5, 2013).

Slugline, computer software, available at http://slugline.co (accessed December 5, 2013).

StorySkeleton, computer software, available at http://www.storyskeleton. com (accessed December 5, 2013).

DOI: 10.1057/9781137469816.0016

Talvio, Raija. 2014. 'Screenwriting without Typing—The Case of Calamari Union', *Journal of Screenwriting* 5 (1): 85–100.

Trottier, David. 2010. *The Screenwriter's Bible: A Complete Guide to Writing, Formatting, and Selling Your Script*, 5th edn. Los Angeles, CA: Silman-James Press.

Waldeback, Zara and Batty, Craig. 2012. *The Creative Screenwriter: Exercises to Expand Your Craft*. London: Methuen.

DOI: 10.1057/9781137469816.0016

Part IV
The Self

Berry, Marsha and Max Schleser. *Mobile Media Making in an Age of Smartphones*. New York: Palgrave Macmillan, 2014. DOI: 10.1057/9781137469816.0017.

▶

Much of the early research into mobile phones exposes the ways in which mobile phones penetrate everyday social interactions and rituals including our self-presentation. Brown, Green, and Harper (2002) discuss the way in which the popularity of the mobile phone surprised computer science researchers who did not imagine that people would engage with such small screens. Ito and Okabe, writing in 2005, saw mobile phones as a technology that changes the way people interact with each other. They suggested rethinking and reframing previous definitions of social situations to include technosocial dimensions. Furthermore, they proposed that boundaries of identity and the self needed to be redrawn to accommodate technological infrastructures that facilitate the development of new social norms. Ling (2004), an established theorist in the use of mobile phones, proposed that mobile phones reconfigure social rituals and facilitate social cohesion.

Arguably, mobile phones have had an immense impact on norms of self-presentation and in turn this has generated new practices that affect every aspect of our lives. In this section the essays engage with how social rituals and constructions of the self are being reconfigured in an age of smartphones and social media. Abidin exposes how carefully a staged online self can be used to create online celebrity status and financial gain. Selfies have become big business and are highly crafted by Singaporean bloggers. She shows how self-presentation may be leveraged into new financially lucrative creative forms through smartphones and social media.

There are claims that the Internet is rewiring our brains and that 'our life is fastfood, fast media, fast cars and a fast cycle to crash and burn' (Carr 2008). A phenomenon called 'slow media' has arisen as a response. The rise of slow media may be interpreted as a response to the need to slow down. A Google search of 'slow media' shows numerous blog posts discussing the effects and affects of switching off or reducing one's consumption and use of media. It is part of a broader social zeitgeist including the slow food movement, slow art, slow writing, slow cinema, and slow reading. Kelly expands on debates about the place of mobile media in contemporary life. His chapter uses the slow movement as its point of reference and explores how autoethnography may be adopted as a methodology for exploring the implications of smartphones for filmmaking practices. His chapter focusing on the self as both the subject and object of his inquiry provides valuable insights for creative practice research strategies.

DOI: 10.1057/9781137469816.0017

Self-portraits have been a subject for creative practice for many generations but a new visual genre has emerged around smartphone practices of sharing selfies through social media apps, according to Jerry Saltz in his recent article in *Vulture*. This new visual genre is distinguished by its spontaneity and casualness. He claims that selfies 'have changed aspects of social interaction, body language, self-awareness, privacy, and humor, altering temporality, irony, and public behavior' and that as a genre the selfie is 'in its Neolithic phase' and 'has already mutated at least once'. He concludes his article by saying that 'we will one day see amazing masters of the form'.

Goméz Cruz and Miguel's chapter explores the role smartphone cameras play in intimacy. Whether texting and sexting harm or enhance relationships is an open question. Gregoire (2013) from Huffington Post reported that a quantitative survey study by 'researchers at Brigham Young University recently found heavy texting to be associated with relationship dissatisfaction among both men and women' (Gregoire 2013, n.p.). The study by Schade et al. (2013) found that texting could inhibit strong emotional connections in couples as well as interrupt in person encounters. Goméz Cruz and Miguel present a more nuanced ethnographic study that exposes some of the private aspects of selfies and mediating the self in romantic and sexual relationships and show how new forms of intimate social interaction through photography are being normalized.

Selfies, as Schleser observes in his chapter in this section, are all about the present tense. Many are not taken for posterity; rather their function can be to engage in conversations that are taking place at a particular moment on social media timelines. His chapter engages with dialogues about the place of smartphones in first-person filmmaking practices showing that selfies and documentaries made on smartphones not only produce new genres but also extend autobiography as a creative practice.

References

Brown, Barry, Green, Nicola and Harper, Richard. 2002. *Wireless World: Social and Interactional Aspects of the Mobile Age*. London: Springer-Verlag.

DOI: 10.1057/9781137469816.0017

Carr, Nicholas 2008. 'Is Google Making Us Stupid? What the Internet is doing to our Brains', *The Atlantic*, http://www.theatlantic.com/magazine/archive/2008/07/is-google-making-us-stupid/6868/ (accessed May 30, 2014).

Gregoire, Caroline. 2013. 'Too Much Texting Could Be Harming Your Relationship, Study Finds', *Huffington Post*, http://www.huffingtonpost.com/2013/11/01/too-much-texting-could-be_n_4192051.html (accessed May 30, 2014).

Ito, Mizuko and Okabe, Daisuke. 2005. 'Technosocial Situations: Emergent Strcuturing of Mobile and e-mail Use', in Mizoko Ito et al. (eds), *Personal, Portable, Pedestrian*. Cambridge: MIT Press.

Ling, Rich. 2004. *The Mobile Connection: The Cell Phone's Impact on Society*. San Francisco, CA: Morgan Kaufman.

Saltz, Jerry. 2014. 'At Arms Length: A History of the Selfie', *Vulture*, http://www.vulture.com/2014/01/history-of-the-selfie.html (accessed July 5, 2014).

Schade, Lori, Cluff, Sandberg, Jonathan, Bean, Roy, Busby, Dean and Coyne, Sarah. 2013. 'Using Technology to Connect in Romantic Relationships: Effects on Attachment, Relationship Satisfaction, and Stability in Emerging Adults', *Journal of Couple & Relationship Therapy: Innovations in Clinical and Educational Interventions*, 12 (4): 314–338. DOI: 10.1080/15332691.2013.836051

DOI: 10.1057/9781137469816.0017

11

#In$tagLam: Instagram as a Repository of Taste, a Burgeoning Marketplace, a War of Eyeballs

Crystal Abidin

▶

Abstract: *Bloggers in Singapore are fast becoming Asia's upcoming generation of lucrative entrepreneurs, some with earnings rolling into the millions. Through 'lifestyle blogs' containing personal diary entries interwoven with personalized advertorials and paid reviews, their private lives become a tool for selling products and services, and this manufactured celebrity has in recent years begun to be broadcast on other social media enterprises. Among these, Instagram is the fastest growing media application among mobile-savvy users in Singapore (TNP September 1st, 2013). As a result of these emergent practices, entanglements such as the ownership of hashtags, competitive strategies to be featured on Instagram's 'Popular Page', and tagging 'wars' have begun to circulate within an industry where personal lives are real-time billboards to eager, watchful eyeballs.*

Berry, Marsha and Max Schleser. *Mobile Media Making in an Age of Smartphones.* New York: Palgrave Macmillan, 2014. DOI: 10.1057/9781137469816.0018.

DOI: 10.1057/9781137469816.0018

A silver tray of finger food has finally arrived at our table during a bloggers-only launch party for a new candy. Almost immediately, cameras and smartphones are whipped out and aimed at the tray. Emma's boyfriend and I are the only nonbloggers at the table. He instinctively shifts our drinks away from his 24-year-old girlfriend's line of sight, then, before I can reach for the food, turns to me and says, 'wait for them to *Instagram* first'.

Ryan and I are in a cab to dinner with several bloggers. Mid-sentence, the 18-year-old's cell phone alarm blares, reminding him to publish an Instagram photo. 'Sorry ah, I need to *Instagram* now', he says, cutting short our conversation as he flips through photograph filters on the app. The photo of him posing at a sponsored beverage event was shot some days earlier. Yet he tells me that today (Friday) and this time (6 p.m.) is the optimal slot to 'get Instagram likes'.

I watch as Linda extends her arm to position her iPhone over her head. Over and over again, she attempts to capture her designer handbag, new leather bracelet, and limited edition silver rings over her carefully angled 'skinny' thighs. After all, crafting the perfect photograph for her 50,000 followers on Instagram is no easy feat. 'I need natural light', the 19-year-old informs me as she leans toward the window, 'then my Instagram photo will be nice'.

With island-wide Wi-Fi spots (iDA 2013), 87% smartphone penetration (Media Research Asia 2013), and 123% mobile Internet penetration (Singh 2014) for a population of almost 5.4 million (Singstat 2013), Singapore is one of the most 'wired' nations in the world (Tan 2009). Instagram is also the fastest growing media application among mobile-savvy users, with its share of total social site visits growing '8,121 per cent in Singapore between July 2011 and July 2012' (Aw Yeong 2013).

Although designed as an app that spontaneously catalogues one's life 'as they happen' (Instagram 2013a), the three vignettes above showcase Emma, Ryan, and Linda laboring over their photographs to portray a crafted persona. Like many lifestyle bloggers in Singapore since early 2012 (personal notes), they have monetized Instagram as an advertising space.

Instagram is a free photo-sharing smartphone app that requires an Internet or 3G connections. Users may tag their photos into searchable categories by adding the hash key in front of a word or short phrase; this is known as a 'hashtag'. Popular hashtags in Singapore include #ootd, an acronym for Outfit Of The Day, and #igsg, indicating Instagram

DOI: 10.1057/9781137469816.0018

Singapore. Users may 'like' and comment on each other's photograph. Popular users on Instagram are likely to have high follower-to-following ratios, that is, having a large number of users subscribed to their account while themselves subscribing to only a small number of users. Instagram also features a 'Popular Page'—officially known as the 'Explore Tab' (Instagram 2013b)—that showcases 15 trending posts worldwide. Featured users often gain a sizable number of new followers. Many Singaporean bloggers make it to Instagram's 'Popular Page' regularly, even writing 'how to' guides on their blogs.

International news reports reveal how Instagram is used for business, including American retailers hawking wares (Rosenberg 2013), Saudi women selling cosmetics (Ahmad 2014), and Australian women advertising products (Bennett 2014). Scholarly studies have investigated Instagram's use to engage undergraduates in teaching and learning (Salomon 2013), analyze location-based visual information flows (Hochman and Schwartz 2013), communicate the museum experience (Weilenmann et al. 2013), and in photojournalism visually document war (Alper 2013). Caumont describes cell phones as 'the third screen, in addition to television and computers' (Caumont in Goggin 2006, 162) that advertisers are increasingly using to reach their target audience. Following on, this chapter is an ethnographic study of how commercial lifestyle bloggers in Singapore use Instagram for their business.

While they may have made their debut on blogs, commercial lifestyle bloggers are now using Instagram extensively. I refer to them as 'bloggers' rather than 'Instagrammers' for two reasons; first because blogging is the mainstay of their industry, and secondly to differentiate them from web personalities who have a presence solely on Instagram.

Wendy Cheng, better known by her blog persona Xiaxue, is Asia-Pacific's most prolific commercial blogger and the winner of several regional blog awards. As of January 2014, Xiaxue boasts 40,000 daily blog views, 177,000 Twitter followers, and 449,000 Instagram followers. On her blog, she details receiving sponsorship for her house renovation and interior design, valued at an estimated SGD$100,000. She also received a year's use of three different vehicles from a car dealer. In exchange, Xiaxue advertises for the companies on her social media platforms. In most arrangements, bloggers receive payment for advertising. Popular commercial bloggers are usually signed to blog advertising companies—whose managers broker such collaborations and endorsements—while others work freelance. Both groups, however, need to consistently

DOI: 10.1057/9781137469816.0018

maintain their Instagram personas to lure followers, and do so by curating Instagram posts to perform a desirable lifestyle.

The data is drawn from fieldwork undertaken between December 2012 and July 2013. It comprises personal interviews, observations in bloggers' working environments, and observations of bloggers' Instagram feeds. Pseudonyms are used. The chapter has three aims. First, it shows how lifestyle bloggers use Instagram to 'perform' taste. Secondly, it situates Instagram as an innovative medium for advertising in the electronic market place. Thirdly, it investigates bloggers' strategies to increase their viewership. This chapter argues that commercial bloggers labor to manufacture a commercial Instagram persona, to such a degree of calculated performativity that it has evolved into a lifestyle.

Like me! Instagram as a repository of taste

Bloggers maintain their ongoing Instagram personas by publishing photographs deemed congruent with upper-middle-class taste. One of Linda's attractions is her display of luxury items, which she claims incites followers' interest. One post reveals up to SGD$6,000 of leather goods. Linda has a 'megaphone effect' on her viewers, in which ordinary nonprofessional consumers independently publicize their consumption practices, and accumulate a 'mass audience of strangers' (McQuarrie et al. 2013, 137).

Linda rarely reveals her nonluxury items, despite them being the mainstay of her wardrobe 'off Instagram', to channel a 'pecuniary taste'. This borrows from Veblen's notion of 'pecuniary beauty', in which expensive objects are perceived as more desirable and beautiful because people increasingly value wealth (Veblen 1961). Other displays of public consumption and 'pecuniary taste' include holidays to exotic destinations, exclusive dining experiences, or private events with mainstream television and film personalities who are not usually accessible to the public. Like many popular bloggers, however, Linda makes an exception for the low-end mass produced apparel that she models on her Instagram for a fee. Her labor to portray a luxurious Instagram persona obscures the fact that she is actually working for an income.

'Pecuniary taste' here extends to displaying one's sociality and personal networks. Some bloggers only postgroup photographs with fellow commercial bloggers, excluding personal friends who are not

DOI: 10.1057/9781137469816.0018

familiar faces to Instagram followers. These boundary markers embed them within a particular class of successful bloggers, thus establishing the value and exclusivity of their social network.

Evidently for commercial bloggers, using Instagram is less about making 'memor[ies] to keep around forever' (Instagram 2013a) and more about catering to an audience. Ryan often makes quick evaluations of whether a photograph is 'Instagram worthy' based on its projected number of likes. Taking Instagram photos thus becomes less of a leisurely pursuit when bloggers constantly deliberate over the value of an image. As arbiters of taste, some women bloggers even cosmetically manipulate their bodies to channel their perceptions of hegemonic beauty to earn 'likes' and gain followers. For instance, coinciding with the K-Pop wave in Singapore in 2013, many bloggers adopted porcelain skin tones, enlarged dark pupils, and blonde hair. Commercial bloggers thus reflexively critique and discipline their bodies to convey a desirable Instagram persona.

Photo-taking skills are crucial in the industry, as blogger managers refer to it as a talent that is difficult to train, whereas other aspects of the business such as good writing skills and carrying yourself well can be developed. This capacity to create aesthetically pleasing images is an 'inborn taste', to borrow from Veblen's notion of 'inborn beauty' (Veblen 1961). Unlike pecuniary taste, inborn taste is posited as an innate ability. Gronow refers to this as a 'judgment power' (Gronow 1997) that is irrational and arbitrary, although widely agreed upon by most people. Both types of taste are alternative ladders for bloggers to accrue capital, instead of acquiring the traditionally more highly regarded business skills of good writing and networking. Instagram thus becomes a project of self-creation, where bloggers conscientiously hone their public personas as arbiters of taste.

However, what is excluded from bloggers' Instagram is as important as what is emphasized. For instance, Linda's managers advised her not to publish photographs of her clubbing escapades. This was to maintain her 'role model' image to her under-18 followers to whom she frequently markets clothing and affordable cosmetics. Bloggers thus labor over maintaining the congruence of their persona to remain believable to followers. In summary, only bloggers whose Instagram portray a desirable upper-middle-class lifestyle, whose bodies channel hegemonic beauty, and whose persona is congruent, attract a sizable number of followers, and thus, advertisers.

DOI: 10.1057/9781137469816.0018

Buy me! Instagram as a burgeoning market place

Commercial bloggers' aptitude for creating and sustaining social media trends has been monetized by the sale of advertising space. In this process they are exchanging their acquired cultural capital for financial gain. However, this requires maintaining a balance between commerciality and intimacy, and distributing viewership between Instagram and blogs. Followers are most receptive to posts that seamlessly meld into a blogger's daily stream, and lose interest in bloggers who have become too commercialized (Kozinets et al. 2010). Therefore, bloggers must ensure that sponsored posts do not take precedence over 'personal' posts, and avoid 'selling out'. After all, commercial bloggers started out as ordinary people who are more accessible and believable than mainstream celebrities, and whose credibility is based on their ability to relate to the experiences of average consumers. To obscure the commerciality of their business and maintain intimacy with followers, Anna bookends each advert with a 'personal' post, while Irene integrates products into her signature 'selfies' (self-portrait photographs taken with a handheld phone or camera).

By mid-2013, blog readership decreased drastically. Instagram became the most popular social media app. This was detrimental as blogs are more effective than Instagram in terms of selling power, because they allow space for lengthy, detailed advertorials. Ryan laments that his 'Insta [followers] are increasing but blog [viewership] is decreasing'. He is focused on improving his Instagram posts to 'lure readers back' to his blog. Bloggers have begun publishing 'selfie' shots announcing a new blogpost. Hashtags such as #blogged and #ontheblog were introduced to adapt this self-promotion into stylized 'Instagram speak'. These innovations, while appearing like creative wordplay, are in fact deliberate efforts to steer readership toward avenues that are more profitable for bloggers. In general, bloggers have to maintain their Instagram personas without appearing too commercialized. They must develop creative strategies to integrate advertisements into their feed, and redirect Instagram viewership to their blogs to increase their advertising revenue.

Watch me! Instagram as a war of eyeballs

Ryan's calculated release of both commercial and 'personal' Instagram posts is common among bloggers. For followers in the Singapore time

DOI: 10.1057/9781137469816.0018

zone, bloggers identify weekday mornings between 8 and 10 am, and evenings between 7 and 9 pm as 'high traffic' periods. These coincide with the close of business rush hours, when users are not engaged in formal work and use their phones recreationally. Bloggers like Amanda purposely schedule their prospective Instagram posts, and 'save #ootd outfits for good days'. Emma even has a pen-and-paper diary in which she notes which photos to publish weekly. This dependency on apps such as Instagram is why bloggers like Christine have at least two 'fully charged portable battery packs' for her phone. It is also why Yvonne turned down the opportunity for an exotic holiday because the remote island had no data roaming networks. Maintaining an Instagram persona has thus made 'lifestyle' and 'work' one and the same for these bloggers. Their lifestyles are no longer demarcated into formal work hours and recreational nonwork hours because maintaining a congruent Instagram persona necessitates continuous deliberations over all facets of life.

Some bloggers adopt hashtags to wrestle attention from competitors. Unique hashtags circulate their posts across different categories. For instance, if Marie hashtags her photograph with '#ootd #brunch #girl #mariepix' users who explore the feeds of any of the first three globally popular hashtags will also see Marie's posts. On it, they will notice her unique '#mariepix' hashtag and be enticed to click into her personal stream that archives all the posts hashtagged this way. However, creating unique hashtags are only personal and 'exclusive' to the blogger until they become appropriated or 'hijacked' by other users who 'piggy-back' on the success of others' hashtags.

Hijacking is a colloquial term that refers to other users taking advantage of personal hashtag streams by spamming or self-advertising. These infiltrations disrupt bloggers' Instagram personas by breaking the coherence of the lifestyle they perform—at times to the extent that the hashtag is abandoned altogether. Some bloggers publish pleas to play fair or shame unethical users, while others adapt and transform their personal hashtags once they have been made redundant. One example is fictional blogger Mary Anne Lim, who would evolve her hashtag from #maryannelim to #MALblogs to #maryannelimsg. Other bloggers create pastiche text with leetspeak (an informal alphabet replacing letters with numerals and characters that is used primarily on the Internet), such as modifying #ootd into #007d. Hence, while it appears frivolous, wrestling for limelight on hashtag streams is in fact a measured process bloggers' use to promote themselves. In summary, bloggers constantly generate new approaches to command the

DOI: 10.1057/9781137469816.0018

attention of their viewers as the industry becomes increasingly saturated. They do so by tactically publishing posts in prime time slots, scheduling posts in advance, and adopting the use of global and personal hashtags.

The #In$tagLam lifestyle

Instagram is a medium through which commercial lifestyle bloggers demonstrate their group membership in the industry, sell advertising space, and maintain viewer interest. While Instagram claims to enable users to share moments 'as they happen', the opening vignettes in this chapter demonstrate bloggers' creative adaptations of Instagram, which have arisen from its commercial appropriation. Be it Emma's predisposition to photographing food, Ryan's deliberations over primetime slots, or Linda's labor over creating perfect (yet seemingly spontaneous) shots, performing commercial personas on Instagram is strenuous because a lot of effort is needed to 'manufacture' a persona that is desirable. In fact, this labor requires such a degree of calculated performativity that it has evolved into a lifestyle.

Commercial bloggers labor to portray a desirable upper-middle-class lifestyle and channel hegemonic ideals of beauty through their bodies. This attracts viewers to vicariously experience their lives by subscribing to their Instagram feed. To maintain viewer interest, they appropriate creative strategies to obscure the commerciality of their posts. They also redirect the attention they receive on Instagram to their blogs to increase advertising revenue. As the industry becomes increasingly saturated, bloggers constantly generate approaches to compete for the attention of viewers. To do so, they labor over prime time slots, scheduling posts, and the use of hashtags. They also maintain their smartphone's battery life and Internet connection in order to be constantly connected to Instagram. Bloggers who successfully capture an audience who will 'Like them', 'Buy them', and 'Watch them' will have long careers in the industry.

References

Ahmad, Hayat Ali. 2014. ' "Instagram Shopping" a Hit with Young Saudi Entrepreneurs', *Arab News*, January 11. http://www.arabnews.com/news/507381 (accessed January 15, 2014).

DOI: 10.1057/9781137469816.0018

Alper, Meryl. 2013. 'War on Instagram: Framing Conflict Photojournalism with Mobile Photography apps', *New Media & Society*, 1–16. Published online at http://nms.sagepub.com/content/early/2013/09/16/1461444813504265 (accessed January 6, 2014).

Aw Yeong, Benita. 2013. 'Instagram is Fastest Growing Media Application among Mobile-savvy Users Here', *The New Paper*, September 1. http://www.tnp.sg/content/instagram-fastest-growing-media-application-among-mobile-savvy-users-here (accessed January 15, 2014).

Bennett, Stephanie. 2014. 'Renee Somerfield Turns Instagram Selfies into Big Business', *Courier Mail*, January 17. http://www.couriermail.com.au/news/queensland/renee-somerfield-turns-instagram-selfies-into-big-business/story-fnihsrf2-1226803573420 (accessed January 20, 2014).

Goggin, Gerard. 2006. *Cell Phone Culture: Mobile Technology in Everyday Life*. London: Routledge.

Gronow, Jukka. 1997. *The Sociology of Taste*. London: Routledge.

Hochman, Nadav and Rax Schwartz. 2013. 'Visualizing Instagram: Tracing Cultural Visual Rhythms', *AAAI Technical Report WS-12-03 Social Media Visualization*. http://www.aaai.org/ocs/index.php/ICWSM/ICWSM12/paper/viewFile/4782/5091 (accessed January 6, 2014).

iDA Infocomm Development Authority of Singapore. 2013. 'Wireless@SG'. http://home.singtel.com/hotspot/wirelesssg/login.asp (accessed January 5, 2014).

Instagram. 2013a. 'FAQ'. Accessed January 5. http://instagram.com/about/faq/

Instagram. 2013b. 'Explore Tab'. http://help.instagram.com/487224561296752 (accessed January 5, 2014).

Kozinets, Robert V., Kristine de Valck, Andrea C. Wojnicki, and Sarah J. S. Wilner. 2010. 'Networked Narratives: Understanding Word-of-Mouth Marketing in Online Communities', *Journal of Marketing* 74: 71–89. http://content.ebscohost.com/pdf23_24/pdf/2010/JMK/01Mar10/47927924.pdf?T=P&P=AN&K=47927924&S=R&D=ufh&EbscoContent=dGJyMNLe80SeqLE4yNfsOLCmroyeqLBSsqe4SrGWxWXS&ContentCustomer=dGJyMPGpsU22rbdOuePfgeyx44Dt6fIA (accessed January 23, 2014).

Media Research Asia. 2013. '87% Smartphone Penetration In Hong Kong, Singapore'. http://www.mediaresearchasia.com/view.php?type=press&id=3184 (accessed January 5, 2014).

DOI: 10.1057/9781137469816.0018

McQuarrie, Edward F., Jessica Miller and Barbara J. Phillips. 2013. 'The Megaphone Effect: Taste and Audience in Fashion Blogging', *Journal of Consumer Research* 40(1): 136–158. http://www.jstor.org/stable/10.1086/669042 (accessed January 23, 2014).

Rosenberg, Joyce M. 2013. 'Instagram and Pinterest are Getting likes from Business Owners', *Financial Post*, December 23. http://business.financialpost.com/2013/12/23/instagram-and-pinterest-are-getting-big-likes-from-business-owners/ (accessed January 15, 2014).

Salomon, Danielle. 2013. 'Moving on from Facebook: Using Instagram to Connect with Undergraduates and Engage in Teaching and Learning', *College & Research Libraries News* 74(8): 408–412. http://crln.acrl.org/content/74/8/408.short (accessed January 6, 2014).

Singh, Shelley. 2014. 'Mobile Internet Boom Coming, but Challenges Remain', *The Times Of India*, January 12. http://timesofindia.indiatimes.com/articleshow/28703982.cms (accessed January 15, 2014).

Singstat Department of Statistics Singapore. 2013. 'Latest Data'. http://www.singstat.gov.sg/statistics/latest_data.html#14 (accessed January 5, 2014).

Tan, Weizhen. 2009. 'S'pore is most wired nation', *Asia One*, February 20. http://news.asiaone.com/News/the+Straits+Times/Story/A1Story20090220-123246.html (accessed January 15, 2014).

Veblen, Thorstein. 1961. *The Theory of the Leisure Class.* New York: Random House.

Weilenmann, Alexandra, Thomas Hillman and Beata Jungselius. 2013. 'Instagram at the Museum: Communicating the Museum Experience through Social Photo sharing', *Proceedings of the SIGCHI Conference on Human Factors in Computing Systems*: 1843–1852. http://dl.acm.org/citation.cfm?id=2466243 (accessed January 6, 2014).

DOI: 10.1057/9781137469816.0018

12

Slow Media Creation and the Rise of Instagram

Patrick Kelly

Abstract: *Videography has become synonymous with a modern utilization of the Internet and the most contemporary digital media equipment. The development and rapid uptake of platforms and applications to capture and share video are generating emergent practices associated with social media, presenting new opportunities for filmmakers to explore different contexts. This chapter examines the development of mobile video applications and their use as production tools for the creation of media works embracing the notions within The Slow Media Manifesto. In doing so, it affirms the mobile video format's ability to engage in thoughtful and reflective media creation through the use of applications such as Instagram.*

Berry, Marsha and Schleser, Max. *Mobile Media Making in an Age of Smartphones.* New York: Palgrave Macmillan, 2014. DOI: 10.1057/9781137469816.0019.

This chapter will examine the development of mobile applications and their use as tools for the creation of works that present a context for the self. These works, therefore, embrace the notions surrounding 'The Slow Media Manifesto', with particular reference to the manifesto's call for media to exude a sense of aura. Investigating the debate over the ability for mobile works to generate auratic work, I will review the work of Walter Benjamin (1931, 1935), Jay Bolter (2006), and Stefan Schutt and Marsha Berry (2011). As part of my examination of auratic experience, I will also discuss the presence of 'additional contexts generated through visual juxtapositioning' (Schutt and Berry 2011, 39–40). I will also call on my own autoethnographic and practice-led research to affirm mobile photography and videography's ability to engage in thoughtful and reflective media creation through the use of applications such as Instagram. In doing so, I will identify the potential for these applications to enable auratic experiences and thereby force us to reconsider the mobile's presentation of the self.

The art of image-making has become synonymous with a modern utilization of the Internet and the most contemporary media equipment, with digital technology 'permeat[ing] the entire culture' (Weil 2002, 523). More recently, this development within the areas of production and distribution has spread into the realm of mobile, with some traditional filmmakers even adopting mobile devices in their endeavors. Myers points to South Korean film director Park Chan-wook, who has begun to use the iPhone in his practice, writing that it is the:

> flexibility that is attracting filmmakers to the smartphone as a work tool. If you know what you are doing you can whip out your phone, shoot a scene pretty much anywhere and Bam! It's in the can and ready to be edited. (Myers 2012)

Of course, mobile video-sharing platforms Instagram Video and Vine make this process even easier, to the point where nonprofessional users present themselves online, shooting, editing, and distributing, all within the application. There is a fierce competition generating between the two platforms, operated by Facebook and Twitter respectively, with heated debate also brewing among social media commentators (Talreja 2013). Interestingly the discussion is not centered on the respective features of each application, but rather on the cultures surrounding them, with Xeni Jardin tweeting that 'the vernacular video format emerging on Vine, stuff in the "most popular" list, is fascinating. That pop art form took

DOI: 10.1057/9781137469816.0019

no time to develop (Jardin 2013). As soon as Instagram released video-sharing capabilities, Vine users responded on Twitter using the hash tag #TeamVine to show their loyalty to the perceived Vine community. Instagram is also building a culture around its video sharing through its mission statement 'to capture and share the world's moments' (Buchanan 2013), thereby inferring that its collective users share their own moments with the world. My own Instagram account, for instance, can be utilized to trace my own experiences—ranging from the food I eat and the friends I spend time with, to the work I do and the places to which I travel.

Adding to the public chorus of wide adoption of these contemporary methods is the Tribeca Film Festival, which recently opened a sub-competition, making 'a call for submissions from filmmakers who'd like to use the Vine platform to be featured on TribecaFilm.com, along with a nice cash prize of [US]$600' (Crook 2013). The endorsement of mobile video sharing by Tribeca is a particularly apt one, which demonstrates the progress toward contemporary methods that is so prevalent throughout the film industry, and highlights the professional adoption of typically consumer forms.

There is an argument, however, that these modern techniques of production and distribution are diminishing the ability for media works to engender an aura, a key feature of the Slow Media movement. 'The Slow Media Manifesto' encourages the production of media that generate a feeling that the particular medium belongs to just that moment of the user's life' (David, Blumtritt, and Köhler 2010), a notion that is also inherent in the Slow Food Movement. A significant example of an auratic Slow Food item is lardo di Colonnata, a cured pork product traditionally made in Italy and famous for its white marble. Petrini compared lardo to 'other objects of significant national heritage, including major works of art or buildings of national architectural note' (Leitch in Halpern 2010, 40). Similarly, members of the Slow Media Movement urge producers of media to create work that has auratic qualities and for consumers to ingest such work. This desire for aura, however, is not unique to the Slow movement. In his article 'Everyone I Know is Stayin' Home: The New Cinephila' (2009), James Quandt adds to Sontag's 'lament for the bygone days of cinephilia...' (Betz 2010, 130), writing:

> The phrase "in cinema experience" has recently entered the discourse of film curation—to differentiate traditional filmgoing from gallery and installation presentation of "moving image" works, videotheques, etc.—a marker of the rapid move of cinema's realm from the social and ceremonial to the insular

DOI: 10.1057/9781137469816.0019

and domestic, the analogue to the digital, the hard-won to the easily accessible. (Quandt 2009, n.p.)

Cinephilia's main concern is with the rise of modern technology and its command of the traditional experience of watching a film, projected from celluloid, in a cinema. Quandt uses the example of how the color grade in a 35-mm reel of Jacques Demy's *Model Shop* (1969) was much more vibrant than a DVD version of the same film (Quandt 2009). He claims that the DVD is an inferior copy that lacks the aura of the celluloid version, saying that:

> [o]ne enters the realm of the ineffable, of those venerable Benjaminian notions of aura and authenticity, when attempting to analyze the difference between analogue and digital copies—the weight, solidity, grain, clarity, the there-ness of images are all difficult qualities to describe. (Quandt 2009, n.p.)

He claims that motion picture, edited, manipulated, and printed on celluloid, is an auratic form of art. It could be argued that such an analogy might be additionally applied to the act of sifting through one's news feed on Instagram. Benjamin famously defined aura, in all its slipperiness, as:

> A peculiar web of space and time: the unique manifestation of a distance, however near it may be. To follow, while reclining on a summer's noon, the outline of a mountain range on the horizon or a branch, which casts its shadow on the observer until the moment or the hour partakes of their presence—this is to breathe in the aura of these mountains, of this branch. (Benjamin 1931, 20)

Benjamin's definition arguably raises the question of its own viability. He himself had explanations of events and instances that could and could not bear an aura, ideas that can be shown to directly contradict each other in his various works. In 'The Work of Art in the Age of Mechanical Reproduction', he wrote:

> One might subsume the eliminated element in the term 'aura' and go on to say: that which withers in the age of mechanical reproduction is the aura of the work of art. This is a symptomatic process whose significance points beyond the realm of art. One might generalize by saying: the technique of reproduction detaches the reproduced object from the domain of the tradition. (Benjamin 1935, 3)

Yet, in 'A Short History of Photography', he claims that some earlier photographs produced with 'primitive' cameras had an aura to them, but

DOI: 10.1057/9781137469816.0019

that this aura dissipated upon the introduction of 'instruments capable of overcoming darkness completely and of registering objects with the clarity of a mirror' (Benjamin 1931, 19)—instruments widely used in art in the 1930s. What Benjamin claims is that, the ability to adjust the aesthetics of an image—through such in-camera features as focus, aperture, exposure—renders it unauratic. It could be posited that if Benjamin were writing today, such features might include jump-cut editing features in Vine or retro filters within Instagram.

Few theorists concerned with aura concede that modern works of their time do provoke an aura. Bolter and his colleagues point to *The Oakland Project* (2004), an ongoing audio project based in a cemetery, which offers 'an experience in which visitors walk among the graves and hear the stories of the ghosts' (Bolter et al. 2006, 23), noting that 'we are seeking to exploit the unique character, the aura, of the cemetery' (Bolter et al. 2006, 23). Regarding aura in new media, Bolter and his colleagues write that:

> Benjamin was wrong if he thought audiences and producers would accept a final and irrevocable loss of aura in their popular media forms. What Benjamin identified was not the end of aura, but rather an ongoing crisis, in which the experience of aura is alternatively called into question and reaffirmed. (Bolter et al. 2006, 22)

This explains, then, both Quandt's claim that cinema is auratic and Benjamin's own contrasting views in his various publications: that there is a possibility for contemporary media to exude an aura. Bolter and his colleagues highlight the argument, its reflective nature, and the importance of the experience a viewer has with the artifact in question.

Schutt and Berry (2011) discuss the presence of aura within family photography, quoting Briggs, who wrote that 'the aura is neither a stable attribute nor an object, but an index of the dynamic fraught relationship between the beholder and the artefact' (Briggs in Schutt and Berry 2011, 48). This is an important point, reaffirming Benjamin's contested definition of the term, while also explaining that aura occurs within the connection between the consumer and the object. Schutt and Berry position their own ancestral photographs within the article, noting in two pictures that 'the aura in these two images speaks of optimism and trust in a good future' (Schutt and Berry 2011, 49), thereby indicating that photography can, in fact, exude an aura. What must occur for an aura to be present, they claim, is a personal context,

DOI: 10.1057/9781137469816.0019

of which the viewer is aware and which '...draws our attention to something purportedly embedded in the photo itself, something that we feel but can't put our finger on—the "different intensity"' (Schutt and Berry 2011, 39).

I contend that such personal context is something that has the ability to be present in Instagram images, for makers and viewers alike. Ronnie Scott points to Susan Sontag's argument that to photograph another person means partaking in their mortality, vulnerability, and mutability, then goes on to say that Instagram has us:

> exploring these same qualities in ourselves. Instagram is somewhere between a public broadcast and a diary, so it goes deeper inside its subjects than the photos Sontag was referring to, and reports its finding to a wider audience than photos have before. (Scott 2013, n.p.)

Schutt and Berry highlight the power of juxtaposition and the impact it has on the beholder of an image. They link this 'different intensity' to concepts of postmemory and aura, asserting that '...there are the additional contexts generated through visual juxtapositioning; placing two or more media items together in a visual manner' (Schutt and Berry 2011, 40). Weil recalls the history of juxtaposition 'beginning with collage in the early 20th Century...' and notes that '...as the flow intensifies, artists of all backgrounds have engaged with the notion of reprocessing cultural fragments, thus creating a new context for the comprehension of information...' (Weil 2002, 524).

This notion of context and juxtaposition is demonstrated in many Instagram accounts and feeds, through composing careful sequences of images. Schutt and Berry (2011) write that:

> when someone reads or views a narrative sequence, the meanings they get from, or give to, an item such as a photograph will depend on what came before it and/or after it in the sequence. In other words, new possibilities...are generated from the contexts and frames created by the narrative journey to that item.... (Schutt and Berry 2011, 39)

This concept of juxtaposition, of course, is an important one to consider within the realm of mobile video sharing. In the cases of both Instagram and Vine, while a user's posts are more often separated within a user's news feed, their entire collection of posts can be viewed once a viewer visits their profile. It is in this instance that the importance of juxtaposition within these platforms becomes evident and ample reflection on a user's work can be enacted.

DOI: 10.1057/9781137469816.0019

In the case of Instagram Video, for instance, it is the archiving of captured moments, and the juxtaposition of these moments, that might generate an aura. Instagram's co-founder and CEO, Kevin Systrom says, 'When I think about what Instagram is, I think about moments...Our mission is to capture and share the world's moments' (Buchanan 2013). It is from the context of these captured moments that an auratic experience can emerge. My own Instagram account (@patcheskelly), for instance, demonstrates the ability for mobile platforms to generate a feeling of aura, particularly in a series of videos I shot for the production of an interactive documentary titled *North*. The film was to document my experience of Melbourne, originally as a visitor and then as a resident. From an Instagrammer's perspective, the convenience of utilizing a mobile device offers a filmmaking experience that is unattainable when using more traditional technologies. The portability and high-functionality of both the device and platform mean that images can be captured promptly and inconspicuously with minimal effort, and therefore offer a more personal experience for the capturer. As such, it was not difficult to capture moments and spaces that I found significant with ease and in a short amount of time.

Regarding the moments and places that I did capture, the context of each will differ from viewer to viewer. There are clips captured on the suburban street on which I live, for instance, which is most likely unrecognizable and insignificant to many. On the other hand, of course, there were many locations captured that have their own contexts steeped in a long history, such as the area outside Flinders Street Station and the statues of former political leaders. By collecting a variety of such clips, there emerge many contexts within this series. To invoke Bolter and his colleagues' discussion of *The Oakland Project*, I sought to exploit 'the unique character, the aura' of these locations, as well as my own personal contexts, in an effort to exude an aura from this work, even if certain contexts often remain vague in potentially auratic works: what Schutt and Berry characterize as a feeling that cannot be articulated.

While some viewers may struggle to unveil a context to some of the images in the series, Pink highlights an appreciation for personal subjectivities, writing:

> More recently, MacDougall (1997) proposed that ethnographic documentary film should be used to challenge objectifying approaches in anthropology to emphasize the experiential and individual nature of social life and develop

DOI: 10.1057/9781137469816.0019

> its potential to represent individuals and specific aspects of experience. This
> approach informs a style of filmmaking in which individuals rather than
> 'whole cultures' dominate and the subjectivities of both filmmakers and
> subjects are appreciated. (Pink 2001, 139)

It is also worth noting that, as an ongoing and often-utilized account
to which I will continue to post images, I expect that many of these
contexts will grow stronger and more explicit in time. Furthermore,
to isolate just one or a handful of videos on any particular Instagram
feed would be to limit the potential for many contexts to emerge. It is
through viewing the videos made for the *North* project together that one
might gain an understanding of my experience of Melbourne. Likewise,
it is through exploring the rest of the account that one might fathom the
other experiences of my life; the food I eat; the places I go; the work I
do; the jokes I find funny; the beliefs I hold; the relationships I have; the
successes I achieve; the losses I face.

The ability for contemporary mobile platforms to present such
contexts to its users indicates that their images can exude aura. As
Bolter points out, the fact that contemporary media technologies
are used in the production of a work does not disqualify that work
from being auratic. In fact, it is in these platforms' juxtapositioning
nature that one might discover the emergence of even more contexts
and auratic experiences. As such, users of Instagram and Vine have
the ability to produce works that are aligned with 'The Slow Media
Manifesto', thus forcing us to reconsider mobile platforms' impact on
notions of self.

References

Benjamin, Walter. 1931. *A Short History of Photography*. Translated
by Phil Patton. New York, NY: Artforum 15(6), 1977. http://
imagineallthepeople.info/Benjamin.pdf.

Benjamin, Walter. 1935. *The Work of Art in the Age of Mechanical
Reproduction*. Translated by Harry Zohn. New York, NY: Schocken
Books, 1969. http://web.mit.edu/allanmc/www/benjamin.pdf.

Benjamin, Walter. 1972. 'A Short History of Photography', *Screen* 13 (1):
5–26.

DOI: 10.1057/9781137469816.0019

Betz, Mark. 2010. 'In Focus: Cinephilia – Introduction'. *Cinema Journal* 49 (2): 130–132.

Bolter, Jay David, Blair Macintyre, G., Maribeth Y. and Petra Schweitzer. 2006. 'New Media and the Permanent Crisis of Aura', *Convergence: The International Journal of Research into New Media Technologies* 12 (1): 21–39.

Buchanan, Matt. 2013. 'Instagram and the Impulse to Capture Every Moment', *The New Yorker*, June 20. http://www.newyorker.com/ online/blogs/elements/2013/06/instagram-videos-and-the-impulse-to-capture-every-moment.html (accessed 30 July, 2013).

Crook, Jordan. 2013. 'Tribeca Film Festival Narrows Down #6SecFilms Submissions to a Short List of 40 Awesome Vines", TechCrunch.com, April 17. http://techcrunch.com/2013/04/17/tribeca-film-festival-narrows-down-6secfilms-submissions-to-a-short-list-of-40-awesome-vines/ (accessed September 9, 2013).

David, Sabria, Jörg Blumtritt, and Benedikt Köhler. 2010. 'The Slow Media Manifesto'. Slow-Media.net. Published January 2. http://en.slow-media.net/manifesto.

Digital Afro. 2003. 'Instagram Video vs Vine?... Which One Is Better? We Break It Down'. http://www.digitalafro.com/instagram-video-vs-vine-which-one-is-better-we-break-it-down/ (accessed January 8, 2014).

Myers, Tony. 2012. 'Lights, action... iPhone? Filmmakers turn to smartphones', *The Guardian*, February 9. http://www.guardian.co.uk/technology/blog/2012/feb/09/filmmakers-turn-to-smartphones (accessed 5 April, 2013).

Pink, Sarah. 2001. *Doing Visual Ethnography*. London: Sage.

Quandt, James. 2009. 'Everyone I Know is Stayin' Home: The New Cinephilia'. Framework: *The Journal of Cinema and Media* 50 (1&2). http://findarticles.com/p/articles/mi_7139/is_200904/ai_n52370152/ (accessed April 6, 2010).

Schutt, Stefan and Marsha Berry. 2011. 'The Haunted Photograph: Context, Framing and the Family Story', *Current Narratives* 1 (3): 35–53.

Scott, Ronnie. 2013. 'Face Value', *Meanjin*. http://meanjin.com.au/articles/post/face-value/ (accessed May 14, 2014).

Talreja, Prerna. 2013. 'Instagram Video vs. Vine: Why Vine Will Emerge on Top', Polymic.com, July 3. http://www.policymic.com/

DOI: 10.1057/9781137469816.0019

articles/52653/instagram-video-vs-vine-why-vine-will-emerge-on-top (accessed 30 July, 2013).

Weil, Benjamin. 2002. 'Art in Digital Times: From Technology to Instrument', *Leonardo* 35 (5): 523–537.

DOI: 10.1057/9781137469816.0019

13

I'm Doing This Right Now and It's for You. The Role of Images in Sexual Ambient Intimacy

Edgar Gómez Cruz and Cristina Miguel

▶
Abstract: *The purpose of this chapter is to present some thoughts on how photographic practices are part of an increasing normalization of intimate mediations by forming specific assemblages (see Rose, 2014) of text, connectivity, seduction, and timing. We will focus specifically on sexually mediated practices, since these seem to be a fertile ground to analyze how the normalization of these intimate mediations is being shaped. The chapter reports on an ongoing research agenda that focuses on photography as a series of practices in everyday life and goes beyond focusing solely on what is depicted in the images. Concepts addressing sex and mediated communications and discuss practices related to digital images such as selfies and sexting are situated within a wider discussion on visuality, mobility, and everyday practices.*

Berry, Marsha and Max Schleser. *Mobile Media Making in an Age of Smartphones.* New York: Palgrave Macmillan, 2014. DOI: 10.1057/9781137469816.0020.

V., a woman in her thirties is having a lunch break in her office. Her boyfriend is in another country and, due to the different time zones he's ready to go to bed. They start to talk in flirtatious and seductive ways and the conversation, using Whatsapp, reaches a sexual tone. She goes to the toilet and sends him a picture of her breasts while he tells her sweet things and sends her a small clip of him touching himself....

The purpose of this chapter is to present some thoughts on how photographic practices are part of an increasing normalization of intimate mediations by forming specific assemblages (see Rose, 2014) of text, connectivity, seduction, and timing. We will focus specifically on sexually mediated practices, since these seem to be a fertile ground to analyze how the normalization of these intimate mediations is being shaped. The chapter reports on an ongoing research agenda that focuses on photography as a series of practices in everyday life and goes beyond focusing solely on what is depicted in the images (see Edwards 2009; Gómez Cruz 2012; Larsen 2008; Rose 2014). This chapter is divided into three parts. In the first, we briefly present some concepts addressing sex and mediated communications and discuss practices related to digital images such as selfies and sexting. The second section presents the results of a series of interviews with Spanish adults in their thirties who have used images to mediate sexual encounters at some point. Their thoughts help us move away from current alarmist discussions about sexting by reflecting on how the role of images in mediated sexual practices is becoming normalized. Finally, in the conclusion, we discuss some of the implications for a wider discussion on visuality, mobility, and everyday practices.

From cybersex to selfies, sexting and visual intimacies

The relationship between mediated-communication technologies and their usages for sexual practices has a long history and is nothing new. From the beginnings of the digital age, there have been discussions about how computer-mediated communication may be used to create spaces of intimacy described more generally as cybersex. And, taking this argument further in time, we could also mention other technologies that were used before digital times to create mediated intimacy such as

DOI: 10.1057/9781137469816.0020

books, letters, telephone, and photography. It is interesting to note how early and widespread moral concerns about cybersex were discussed in a similar way to today's discussions on sexting. Moreover, even before the arrival of digital technologies, multiple accounts and phrases to denote the production and circulation of imagery to create sexual intimacy existed (Coopersmith 2000; Edgley and Kiser 1982). What seems to be new is the convergence of digitally mediated communication and ease with which we can distribute images. This combination directly impacts on the scale and ease of these practices. Especially significant seems to be the convergence of three key features: mobility, constant connection, and visuality.

When images, Internet connection, and mobility are combined, some practices that were not common previously tend to form new assemblages that are becoming increasingly normalized. We propose that this is the case for so-called selfies, a topic with a growing interdisciplinary interest. Gómez Cruz defines selfies as the 'paradigmatic practice of digital photography' (2012a). Before digital technology, there were self-portraits and they were mostly confined to art photographers or advanced amateur photographers. However, selfies merge the self-portrait vision into an embodied and performative practice whereby images are taken at arm's length or in front of a mirror. This creates a techno-mood that not only enables but also drives users in the direction of intimacy and self-awareness, of tactility and sensuality, and these elements can easily become sexualized.

There seems to be a connection, not yet fully theorized, between selfies and the main talking point regarding the exchange of images of a sexual nature: so-called sexting (see Lenhart 2009). These studies focus mostly on teenagers, detailing the dangers and perils that they could face with these practices. However there is a need to understand these practices beyond the 'danger zone', to better understand how technologies are being used and normalized in mediated sexual practices, it is necessary to widen the scope and avoid the over-simplistic social panic regarding the use of technologies for sexual purposes. Instead we need more research to try to understand how practices that involve sexual imagery are becoming part of flirting and intimate exchanges. Our research addresses the need to extend the discussion around these practices beyond discourses of moral panic in order to explore how these practices are becoming normalized for a number of people.

DOI: 10.1057/9781137469816.0020

Visual intimacies: sex, mobility, and smartphones

Before describing our empirical findings, we focus our attention on the topic of mediated intimacy. As Hjorth and Lim (2012) point out, this can exist between lovers, family members, or close friends, and also between peers and unknown people. As we have previously stated, visuality of (sexual) intimacy seems to be embodied along with physical sensuality (McGlotten 2013) and this is mediated through mobile and digital technologies. The ubiquitous presence of smartphones and the use of social media and exchange platforms allow a constant connection that increasingly relies on the use of visual elements. In their early study about photo sharing through camera phones, Ito and Okabe found out that 'photos tend to be restricted to a more intimate circle of family or lovers' (2005, 1). In 2005, Ito had already identified an emergent visual sharing modality through camera phones in Japan, which she labeled as 'intimate visual co-presence' that she claims is naturally embedded in the intimate nature of mobile devices. Other scholars, such as Thompson (2008) and Hjorth (2012) affirm that this constant social connection through visual experiences over a period of time generates ambient intimacy (Reichelt 2007), which provides the ability for regular intimate relations between people who are separated by time and space. This ambient intimacy could be understood as, for example, constantly knowing banal information about the people you know, such as what your friends had for breakfast. We tweak this concept to focus specifically on the embodied and shared sexual intimacy through smartphones and how this has become a key 'mediated-site' for sexual engagement.

In the age of the smartphones, mobile platforms such as Whatsapp or Snapchat are modifying the traditional flows of intimate visual communication within existing relationships. Immediacy and multi-media capabilities are both keys to the success of these apps. The usage of Whatsapp to send images is popular among smartphone users (Church and Oliveira 2013) and Facebook has just acquired the app for $19 billion. In our study, all participants indicated that they have at some stage used Whatsapp to send erotic pictures to their lovers. One of these informants mentioned that he especially likes Whatsapp because of 'its immediacy, the "I'm doing this right now and it's for you"'. He claimed that he likes to send the same image to two or three people, because 'to see the different reactions to the same image or sexual invitation is a lot of fun'. Snapchat is another app that has been very successful

DOI: 10.1057/9781137469816.0020

for erotic image exchange, especially by teenagers (Poltash 2013). With its focus on the ephemerality of the images (which are auto-destroyed after their visualization) Snapchat claims that, in the social media landscape, it is a 'more-personal' way of communication because it 'focuses on the experience of conversation—not the transfer of information' (Spiegel 2014). Thus, the privacy afforded by the auto-destruction of the visual-messages creates an ideal setting to share intimate experiences that are bounded to specific times, settings, and contexts. Although it is important to note that this ephemerality is not entirely accurate, the important point is that the users have the illusion of it. The relationship between mobility and imagery is extended as well to other intimate practices, such as online dating. There are many mobile apps such as Badoo, PlentyOfFish, Tinder, AdultFriendFinder, or Grindr that are increasingly used to find a partner or to arrange casual sex. For some communities, such as the gay community, these apps are so popular that June Thomas affirms that Grindr might be thought of as the new gay bar (Thomas 2011). In this context the role of the images to foster online and/or offline encounters is paramount and is becoming one of the key elements to intimate interaction.

Visual sexual intimacy

The normalization of visual sexual intimacy, not only seems to be connected with wider transformations in sexual behaviour in Western societies, but also with social and cultural trends such as mobility and communication through digital mediation. Time and space are still important but are being understood in different ways, leading to new forms of mediated intimacy. In reference to the exchange of sexual images with her partner, one informant claimed that: 'I see it normal. I think we all have done it at some point. The eroticism is everywhere: in advertising, in literature…' This is, as a matter of fact, a form of 'particular eroticism. I see my partner in a photo and I get aroused, not only because he is naked but also because he is the person I love'. There is a long history of Western society's exposure to erotic imagery, but these images can now be produced and received by a desired or close person. As another informant mentioned: 'sexual images are still the images that pornography has taught us, but with the add-on of knowing the other person'.

DOI: 10.1057/9781137469816.0020

In a landscape of social mobility, the possibility to be constantly connected increases practices that were seen to be rare before. When talking about her partner who lives in another country, one female informant remarked that: 'while he was extremely against it, "cybersex" was our only way to be intimate to each other'. And another informant, regarding sending pictures to her lover, mentioned: 'I did it to turn him on, to turn myself on, and other times I did it so he didn't forget me when we spent months without seeing each other'. While these sexually intimate encounters seem to become an alternative for sexual partners that are not in the same place, it seems to be a growing part of flirtation practices as well. One of the male informants stated that he does it:

> Because I think is a new interesting way to create and sustain erotic relationships...in my case it is another path for sexual fun...It is great to be able to have sexual or erotic contacts with more than one person despite the distance. It is amazing to be able to create new ways of having sexual experiences.

On the other side of this equation, one woman told the story of meeting a man who tried to engage her in a sexual relationship by 'sending her photos to motivate her'. What is interesting here is that she enjoyed receiving images and knew that he was fond of her but she did not want to have a physically sexual relationship. The same informant mentioned that she began a sexual relationship using this flirtatious 'game' as part of the seduction. This seems to be occurring more since our lives are increasingly lived via our mobile phones; the devices are not only used as mediation tools, but are facilitators in the construction of the ambient intimacy that can sometimes lead to a seductive, erotic, or sexual exchange. In order for this intimacy to be achieved, there seems to be a question of 'shared timing'. This timing could turn an image from a gross invasion to an exciting invitation. What is important, according to one of the key informants, is 'to be sure that the other person wants it too...there is nothing worse than, without any prior warning, suddenly a photo of a guy holding his penis appears on your mobile phone'. She continues:

> The images are part of a conversation, and if you're clumsy in a conversation, you'll be clumsy for every part of that conversation, including images...to turn off a situation there's nothing worse than to be in a hurry. If you're going step by step and suddenly someone sends you an image, it is the same as if you're in a bar talking to someone and suddenly he shows you his penis.

DOI: 10.1057/9781137469816.0020

Our informant concluded by saying, 'I am what I am and I only send pictures when I'm really turned on'. Achieving this moment of arousal through mediated communication requires a combination of elements that contextualize and create this intimate ambience. This is because 'an image has a specific range of qualities as an object, but it is only when someone uses the image in some way that certain of those qualities become activated, as it were, and significant' (Rose 2014, 72). One male informant describes his technique to 'calibrate the empathy' and push this 'activation of qualities' in an image:

> The photo-exchange could begin with something purely casual and funny, such as: 'me in my bed from a subjective point of view' or 'good night, I'm almost sleeping'. If you are more confident, you could send more fun pictures like 'I take off my hat for you' and you send a naked picture of yourself with a hat covering you.

Timing, along with context, shapes the meaning of images that are inserted in a constant communication flow. They are intermingled with words, physical spaces, connections (and disconnections), and this constant exchange creates this ambience of intimacy. Images serve to share not only what is being seen but also what is being imagined. One informant mentioned that she liked to send photos of her body parts 'in the exact same order she would like to be kissed'. Another mentioned that, what she likes about *watching* (someone's body) is *to think* about what she can do with it. Images, along with their textual framing, are not the recipients of meanings or a way to transmit desires; they are a performative mediation between bodies, imagination, cultural codes, time, and space. The mobile phone is at the center of this equation. It is a tool to mediate while performing; a window of endless possibilities.

Conclusions

We have presented some ideas that look to challenge current discussions about sexual imagery exchange. We have proposed a move beyond the image, as such, to explore the wider practices that form assemblages of text, image, connection, time, space, and so on. These assemblages could lead to the creation of a sexual ambient intimacy. People—ordinary people—are experimenting with sexual image exchange as a part of mediated sexual practices due to the ease and availability of cameras

DOI: 10.1057/9781137469816.0020

with Internet connection in smartphones. There are even apps that base their successes on the combination of immediacy, the easy capabilities to share visual and audio files, and the ephemerality of those exchanges.

Interestingly, the ideas and thoughts of people about the exchange of erotic imagery through smartphones are very similar to the findings of an earlier research project about cybersex that one of the authors carried out, at a time when there were no images, just words (Gómez Cruz 2003). Thus, it is also interesting to see how technologies of mediation have seemingly always been used for sexual exchanges. What seems to be new, then, are the multiple possibilities that mobile/visual practices open up. Any space, at any moment, could become an intimate one with the ubiquity of smartphones. These 'always-on/always-on-you' devices, to paraphrase Sheryl Turkle in a humorous way, are increasingly becoming tools for many users to be 'always-*turned*-on'. This phenomenon thus has enormous implications for the ways that we interact with each other: how we shape ourselves; how we build and maintain sexual and social relations; and even how we manage public spaces.

References

Coopersmith, J. 2000. 'Pornography, Videotape and the Internet', *Technology and Society Magazine, IEEE* 19 (1): 27–34.

Church, Karen and Rodrigo de Oliveira. 2013. 'What's up with Whatsapp?: Comparing Mobile Instant Messaging Behaviors with Traditional SMS', in *Proceedings of the 15th International Conference on Human-computer Interaction with Mobile Devices and Services*, 352–361.

Edgley, Charles and Kenneth Kiser. 1982. 'Polaroid Sex: Deviant Possibilities in a Technological Age', *Journal of American Culture* 5 (1): 59–64. doi: 10.1111/j.1542–734X.1982.0501_59.x

Edwards, E. 2009. 'Thinking Photography beyond the Visual?' in J. J. Long, A. Noble and E. Welch (eds), *Photography: Theoretical Snapshots*. London: Routledge, 31–48.

Gómez Cruz, Edgar. 2012a. *De la Cultura Kodak a la imagen en red. Una etnografía sobre fotografía digital*. Barcelona: Editorial UOC.

Gómez Cruz, Edgar and Eric Meyer. 2012. 'Creation and Control in the Photographic Process: iPhones and the Emerging Fifth Moment of Photography', *Photographies* 5 (2): 203–211.

DOI: 10.1057/9781137469816.0020

Gómez Cruz, Edgar. 2003. *Cibersexo: ¿la última frontera del Eros? Un estudio etnográfico*. Colima: Universidad de Colima.

Hjorth, Larissa, Rowan Wilken and Kay Gu. 2012 'Ambient Intimacy: A Case Study of the iPhone, Presence, and Location-based Social Media in Shanghai, China', in L. Hjorth, J. Burgess, and I. Richardson (eds), *Studying Mobile Media: Cultural Technologies, Mobile Communication, and the IPhone*. New York: Routledge, 43–62.

Ito, Mizuko and Daisuke Okabe. 2005. 'Intimate Visual Co-presence'. Paper presented at the Seventh International Conference on Ubiquitous Computing, Tokyo, September 11–14.

Larsen, J. 2008. 'Practices and Flows of Digital Photography: An Ethnographic Framework', *Mobilities* 3 (1): 141–160.

Lenhart, A. 2009. Teens and sexting. *A Pew Internet & American Life Project Report, Retrieved July, 4*, 2010.

McGlotten, Shaka. 2013. *Virtual Intimacies: Media, Affect, and Queer Sociality*. New York: SUNY Press.

Poltash, Nicole A. 2013. 'Snapchat and Sexting: A Snapshot of Baring Your Bare Essentials', *Richmond Journal of Law & Technology* 19 (4): 1–24.

Reichelt, Lisa. 2007. 'Ambient Intimacy', *Disambiguity*, March 1. http://www.disambiguity.com/ambient-intimacy/

Rose, G. 2014. 'How Digital Technologies do Family Snaps, Only Better', in J. Larsen and M. Sandbye (eds), *Digital Snaps: The New Face of Photography*. London: IB Tauris, 67–86.

Spiegel, Evan. 2014. '2014 AXS Partner Summit Keynote', Snapchat Blog, January 27. http://blog.snapchat.com/

Thomas, June. 2011. 'The Gay Bar: Its Riotous Past and Uncertain Future', *Slate Magazine*, June 27, 2011.

Thompson, Clive. 'Brave New World of Digital Intimacy', *The New York Times*, September 7, 2008.

DOI: 10.1057/9781137469816.0020

14

Connecting through Mobile Autobiographies: Self-Reflexive Mobile Filmmaking, Self-Representation, and Selfies

Max Schleser

▶

Abstract: *This chapter examines the recent phenomenon of 'selfies' as a starting point to discuss self-reflexive and self-representation as a narrative strategy within mobile filmmaking. The presented analysis argues that creative mobile media practice can produce representations, which have intimate and immediate characteristics, allowing filmmakers and citizen users to establish new connections with their audiences through digital storytelling. This chapter also establishes a link with the proliferation of mobile filmmaking and the use of mobile camera phones, pocket cameras, and smartphones for self-representation and self-reflexive approaches in mobile filmmaking. It explores mobile devices as a tool for creating self-representation and looks at a user-based interpretation of the autobiographical discourse.*

Berry, Marsha and Max Schleser. *Mobile Media Making in an Age of Smartphones.* New York: Palgrave Macmillan, 2014. DOI: 10.1057/9781137469816.0021.

DOI: 10.1057/9781137469816.0021

This chapter examines the recent phenomenon of 'selfies' as a starting point to discuss self-reflexive and self-representation as a narrative strategy within mobile filmmaking. Furthermore, *Connecting through Mobile Autobiographies* explores the capacities of mobile media for personal storytelling and its significance within the contemporary mediascape.[1] The presented analysis argues that creative mobile media practice can produce representations, which have intimate and immediate characteristics, allowing filmmakers and citizen users to establish new connections with their audiences through digital storytelling. Within this context it is interesting to note that the format of selfies emerged out of online photo-sharing communities which, like mobile filmmaking, are driven through a user-based interpretation of innovation. This chapter also establishes a link with the proliferation of mobile filmmaking and the use of mobile camera phones, pocket cameras and smartphones for self-representation and self-reflexive approaches in mobile filmmaking. The study explores mobile devices as a tool for creating self-representation and looks at a user-based interpretation of the autobiographical discourse.

Connecting through Mobile Autobiographies will provide a brief background to the development of mobile filmmaking as a form of mobile creativity; discussing feature mobile-mentaries (Schleser 2011) (mobile documentaries) produced by mobile pioneers (Lorenzo 2011 online) in the years 2005–2007, the second wave (Schleser 2010, online) of mobile filmmaking (including moving-image and documentary productions by internationally renowned filmmakers and artists from 2007 to 2010), a 2013 public service broadcasting documentary filmed entirely on a smartphone and mobile short films, produced by citizen users, which have been presented at mobile film festivals (Schleser 2013, 93) since 2007. Last year 'selfie' was named the word of 2013 by Oxford Dictionaries, and this now well-established popular culture phenomenon reveals a number of parallels, which are outlined in this chapter, in relation to mobile autobiographies, self-representation, and self-reflexive mobile filmmaking. This chapter illustrates the present tense characteristic for mobile autobiographical filmmaking and proposes that the discussed texts provide a narrative strategy that can capture audiences through their characteristic of establishing personal connections and sociability. In recent years mobile video in its multiple forms and formats has found a resonance in scholarship, mainly dealing with UGC (user-generated content) in mainstream media (such as mobile footage in news broadcasting); this chapter will provide an analysis of the creative practice

DOI: 10.1057/9781137469816.0021

with a focus on self-reflexive mobile filmmaking and autobiographical film theory.

Introduction: toward self-representation

In The Guardian ARTE creative co-production webisode #*Thinkfluencer,*[2] self-acclaimed super-connector, early-adopter, and self-appointed celebrity web guru Nimrod Kamer takes a not-too-serious and refreshing view on a very recent phenomenon that emerged in the mediascape. In 2013 the word 'selfie' was added to the Oxford Dictionaries, and was defined as 'a photograph that one has taken of oneself, typically with a smart-phone or webcam and uploaded to a social media website'.[3] Judy Pearsall, editorial director for Oxford Dictionaries, explained that 'social media sites helped to popularize the term, with the hashtag #selfie appearing on the photo-sharing website Flickr as early as 2004, but usage wasn't widespread until around 2012, when selfie was being commonly used in mainstream media sources' (Pearsall 2013 online). One should add an interesting fact to this statement, which will provide the focus of analysis in this chapter; the most popular digital camera in the Flickr community is the Apple iPhone. The proliferation of a mobile-media creative practice by citizen users, and the dissemination opportunities through networked and social media that has moved into mainstream since the launch of YouTube in 2005, are very closely related to the emergence of the smart-phone, the pocket camera, and international mobile film festivals (Schleser in Daniels et al. 2013). The significance for this chapter is the context of mobile media creativity that reveals self-reflexive notions; similar forms of self-representation and references to autobiographical filmmaking that characterize mobile films produced by citizen users, mobile filmmakers, and broadcasters alike. Most of these texts engage audiences, amateurs, and young filmmakers, and have provided opportunities for communities to establish local connections and illuminate subjects that normally do not receive much media attention.

Dr Thomas Meyer and I presented a joint conference paper at the Visible Evidence conference in 2010[4]; since then we began to analyze mobile-mentaries (mobile documentaries) produced by citizen users and filmmakers alike. The analysis of case studies such as *Hagen lebt*[5] or *Hallo Hand*[6] corresponds to Dockney and Tomaselli's analysis of mobile or cell phone filmmaking. They suggest the term 'cellphilms' in

DOI: 10.1057/9781137469816.0021

Third Screens, Third Cinema, Third Worlds, and Triadomania: examining Cellphilm aesthetics in visual culture, and say that 'what makes cellphilms significant is their accessibility and their organic, potentially disruptive, codes' (Dockney and Thomaselli 2010, 9). Furthermore, the context of self-reflexive, self-representation, and mobile autobiographies leverages personal storytelling in the mainstream media context and can define new formats and creative practices.

As much as text messaging was created by users, the selfie is a digital vernacular that corresponds to the characteristics of mobile-mentaries (mobile documentaries) and their early aesthetics, which are defined as immediate, intimate, private, and personal. 'Mobile devices make the mundane interesting, the everyday confronted, providing a new lens for viewing the world through a new camera vision' (Baker et al. 2009, 119). Davis argues in *Blurring/Breaking (The) News: Between Amateur and Professional Journalism* that 'more specifically, these person–machine interactions reveal the transformation of important cultural notions, especially the boundaries between the individual and the collective, private and public, memory and experience' (David 2010, 89).

Mobile media creativity: Mobile filmmaking

Within the context of mobile filmmaking the work of early mobile film-making pioneers reflects this analysis. *SMS Sugar Man* is a fictional drama using first-person storytelling in most intimate spaces. The experimental mobile moving-image project *Nausea* was inspired by the impressionis-tic imagery of Jean-Paul Sartre's diary. The British filmmaker Matthew Noel Tod tells a personal story constructed from his memory fragments. *Max with a Keitai* is a self-reflexive city film about mobile filmmaking and Japanese metropolitan cities. Writing in *The Cinema of Me—The Self and Subjectivity in First Person Documentary*, Alisa Lebow argues that 'first person film goes beyond simply debunking documentary's claim to objectivity. In the very awkward simultaneity of being subject in and subject of, it actually unsettles the dualism of objective/subjective divide, rendering it inoperative' (Lebow 2012, 5). The mobile filmmakers create mediated experiences as 'acts of personal remembering', which Smith and Watson in *Reading Autobiography* describe as fundamentally social and collective (Smith and Watson, 2001, 26). They argue that experience is already an interpretation of the past and of our place in a culturally and

DOI: 10.1057/9781137469816.0021

historically specific present. While autobiographical analysis is normally placed in the context of a wider social framework (as in the writing of Sidonie Smith and Julia Watson), this analysis points at the personal and local level. Furthermore, Smith and Watson refer to the notion of experience, saying '...we have it. It is ours. The intimacy and immediacy and palpability of our memories tell us so' (Smith et al. 2011, 30).

Mobile self-reflexive filmmaking can be positioned in a personal and local environment and can introduce a discussion in terms of evaluating the characteristics of intimacy and immediacy. These notions emerge from a personal level. Sidonie Smith and Julia Watson argue that memory as a meaning-making process involves the collections of fragments of the experienced past: 'memory is thus both source and authenticator of autobiographical acts' (Smith et al. 2011, 22). Mobile autobiographies are very much in the present, creating a notion of sociability. Furthermore, mobile filmmaking not only emphasizes the moment but also augments the experience.

Renowned filmmakers used mobile devices in innovative ways in the 'second wave of mobile filmmaking'. Again the exemplified projects highlight the self-reflexive approach in mobile filmmaking; *Why Didn't Anybody Tell Me It Would Become This Bad in Afghanistan* is the diary of a soldier and yet also the diary of a filmmaker. The protagonist, the filmmaker, usually stays indoors in his small flat in Amsterdam, his personal space, and memory. Cyrus Frisch uses documentary aesthetics in a psychological reflection.

The work of Joseph Morder, *J'aimerais partager le Printemps avec Quelqu'un,* can be linked to the previously mentioned aesthetic choices and the notion of the everyday. Joseph's project is centered around the French elections in 2007, which merges the notions of private and the public facts and communication forms into one film diary. Adam Kossoff's *Moscow Diary* is based on Walter Benjamin's work (1926–1927). He used Google Maps on his mobile in one hand and Benjamin's diary in the other. *Immobilité* by Mark America references the DIY (do-it-yourself) aesthetic, and as much as the other works makes a point on the development of film language.

For the public service broadcaster SWR in Germany Rose produced *Assembly line Pittance: How union agreements are bypassed* (*Hungerlohn am Fliessband: Wie Tarife ausgehebelt warden*) in 2013. He filmed the undercover documentary on an iPhone, revealing how Mercedes Benz employs temporary contract workers in order to pay lower wages for the same

DOI: 10.1057/9781137469816.0021

work, at a rate of five Euros an hour. Rose did not use the audio feature as the confidentially of the conversation documented in the audio-recordings could be used as a criminal action against him, while anony-mous pictures can be used even in court scenarios. This raises another set of interesting questions, such as ethics—which are, however, beyond the scope of this chapter. Due to this legal framework Rose produced a diary, speaking into his camera in the style of taking a selfie to capture his everyday and personal experience. This documentary shows that mobile filmmaking has reached a standard accepted by broadcasters. Mobile media making in the age of smartphones references precedents in the last decade in terms of the application of mobile media (camera phones) and creative practices in the form of personal storytelling.

Mobile autobiographies

Writing in *Autobiography, Self into Form*, Sandra Frieden explains autobi-ography, saying that it means to 'tell a story about oneself' (Frieden 1983, 40). Philippe Lejeune outlines the main categories of autobiography for texts as personal history, narration, and the depiction of an individual life in *Le pacte autobiographique* (Lejeune 1994, 15). The depiction of the individual life in these short mobile autobiographies represents a personal account in the present tense.

　The strategy of these first-person mobile films is to maintain the present tense, rather than as in literature, which insists on the past. Similar to the argument presented by Michelle Citron in *Home movies and other necessary fictions*, 'we often connect directly to the person behind the lens'. This relationship is present in mobile filmmaking and the chosen mobile films, but 'rarely in commercial film or mainstream cinema' (Citron 1999, 13). Or rather, one should say, in nonpocket cinema. The characteristics of mobile media and mobile-mentary aesthetics reveal a storytelling strategy with which HD (high definition) and 4K cameras cannot compete. Self-reflexive filmmaking, self-representation, and mobile autobiographies can establish a connection with the audience. Vivian Sobchack points at the transformation of media in *Towards a Phenomenology of Nonfictional Film Experience*. She draws on Meunier's examination of interchangeable categories of the 'home-movie', docu-mentary, and fiction film. This conceptualization can be applied to the chosen mobile phone films in a similar manner. 'Our identification is

DOI: 10.1057/9781137469816.0021

certainly as fluid and dynamic…one viewer's fiction may be another's film-souvenir; one viewer's documentary another's fiction' (Sobchack in Gaine and Renov 1999, 253). As referenced in Lebow's quote, the issue of objectivity and subjectivity is not the question here, nor do these films claim universal validity. Self-reflexive filmmaking, self-representation, and mobile autobiographies can create an engagement with their peers and the people involved in the production.

The mobile camera phone, as a personal and intimate medium, allows an immediate formation of subjective expression. The performance of subjectivity in the first-person autobiographical texts implies a self-referential or a self-reflexive modality. Through observation, mediation, and documentation one can engage in creating an objective distance to and from oneself. In order to reach a stage of self-reflectiveness—as Montaigne did in the 17th century using his pen to express his inner thoughts—one needs to be aware of the limitations of the chosen media for observation and documentation. Without a critical engagement one performs in a self-referential mode. One could argue that selfie represents this self-referential notion, but simultaneously a selfie is produced in order to be shared with friends. The depicted location, one's everyday situation, is part of the personal scenario we bring from our private environment to a public online space. It is a first step toward creating a self-representation by active agents. The creative mobile media practice encourages people to engage in their (social) environment and reflect about their lives. As a level of further engagement mobile filmmaking involves the process of reflecting and selecting fragments from everyday life, which are key for framing the experience through a first-person filmmaking approach.

The daily routines are located in the present tense. The notion of place in these examples is closely related to personal character. For mobile filmmakers these will have personal meanings and memories attached. Robin Curtis refers to the localization in her writing on autobiography as 'verorten'. Curtis says that autobiography provides 'insights about where one stands', a localization of the self-project of representing the self and life in audiovisual form. For her, 'the use-value of autobiography as a genre for self-reflection for historical investigation' thus provides a framework to expand the analysis of contemporary mobile autobiographies according to their specific local characteristics. Mobile productions represent fragments of the contemporary localized zeitgeist. Curtis positions the autobiography as a cultural form (Curtis 2006, 79), which can

DOI: 10.1057/9781137469816.0021

be related to the notion of sociability and its agenda as social practice. In mobile filmmaking the pocket camera format can engage audiences and create sociability that HD industry formats cannot account for in our contemporary attention economy (Davenport and Beck 2002). The mobile autobiographies encapsulate the everyday to gain self-awareness about one's social environment. This self-reflexive modality relates to the narrated, a lived experience. The selfie as a micro-autobiography of the moment in the present tense signifies an organic and disruptive code that can express one's position in the mediascape.

Conclusion: Connecting through mobile autobiographies

The creative mobile media practices described in this chapter explore the mobile filmmakers' subjective expressions in close relationship to their everyday life, merging this into a cinematic form and digital story-telling format. The mobile characteristic explored in here criss-crosses social media, mobile photography apps, and communities such as Flickr, citizen-created projects such as short films screened online and at mobile film festivals, mobile-mentary and smartphone feature films and broadcast media produced on mobile devices.

First-person mobile films, mobile-mentaries, and also the selfie, as a creative activity for citizen users, have a tendency to be what one might describe as incomplete and fragmented using existing analytical frameworks, which were developed for mass media rather than mobile media. Simultaneously, these mobile autobiographies have the capacity to create connections. The mobile aesthetic is leveraged into the network and social media environment and creates connections to audiences through self-representation. Audiences can relate to the moving-image projects of mobile filmmakers and citizen users, as these films portray notions of everyday life that encapsulate the self. These mobile autobiographical films mirror the open-endedness of experience; they are encounters with the world. As a narrative strategy mobile media can enable personal and intimate storytelling in a self-reflexive and self-representational style utilizing the mobility and pocket format of mobile devices. This adds a quality to the contemporary mediascape, which can be positioned on the opposite spectrum of 4K digital cinematography and contemporary broadcast cameras.

DOI: 10.1057/9781137469816.0021

As a creative mobile media practice, mobile films, mobile-mentaries, and selfies allow citizen users and filmmakers to engage with their local environment and reflect on their personal conditions through the filmic production and distribution process. Creative mobile media not only can produce self-representation but can also lead toward the proliferation of new formats, such as selfies and the now well-established genre of mobile filmmaking and mobile-mentaries.

Notes

1   The term 'mediascape' implies that contemporary landscapes can be defined as 'mediated places'. The term mediascape originated from a New York exhibition at the Guggenheim Museum in 1996. While video art surfaced in the gallery context, mobile creative practices transcend gallery space boundaries and move into a ubiquitous realm of 'any place'. Within academic discourse mediascape is normally referenced in relation to Appadurai's discussion in *Modernity at Large*. Rather than deconstructing the ideology within the mediascape, this chapter explores the potential for creating personal representations and adding them to the current media environment. Appadurai, A. (1996) 'Disjuncture and difference in the global cultural economy'. In *Modernity at Large* (p. 35) (Minneapolis: University of Minnesota Press). In M. Schleser and G. David (2013) 'Mobile AR—creating augmented experiences', in *Anti-po-des Journal of Design Research* 2 (August). www.anti-po-des-designjournal.org.nz/current-issue/abstracts-and-papers/schleser-david/.

2   #*Thinkfluencer* episode 1: Selfies—video in Guardian Online http://www.theguardian.com/technology/video/2013/aug/29/thinkfluencer-episode-1-selfies-video (accessed March 3, 2014).

3   'Selfie' named by Oxford Dictionaries as the word of 2013. http://www.bbc.co.uk/news/uk-24992393 (accessed March 3, 2014).

4   Visible Evidence XVII. http://www.bumed.org.tr/images/pdf/visibleevidenceprogram.pdf (accessed March 3, 2014).

5   The notion of the everyday is also present in *Hagen lebt* (*Hagen is alive*). The runner-up nominated project at *Clip: 2 Hagener Handy Film Festival, Hagen lebt* (*Hagen is alive*) depicts the city of Hagen. The mobile film does not provide specific reference points that represent the city of Hagen, but rather functions like a personal snapshot of a suburban German town. *Hagen lebt* connects to the audience through its authenticity or using the Walter Benjamin terminology of aura and its 'presence in time and space'. Walter Bejamin (1968). Hannah Arendt, ed.

DOI: 10.1057/9781137469816.0021

'The Work of Art in the Age of Mechanical Reproduction', Illuminations. London: Fontana. pp. 214–218. Furthermore the mobie film signifies the memory of the mobile filmmaker in its present tense. http://clip2-filmfestival.de/

6 *Hallo Hand* (2007 Raudnitzky) shows the small city of Weiterstadt through the mobile camera of a 'hand-y-man'. Everything within the reach of the filmmaker's arm length is explored in a tactile sense, while simultaneously establishing a notion of presence through the notion of touch. The project was part of the *Mobile Movie School* at the 31st *Open Air Filmfests* Weiterstadt. Hallo Hand (2007 Raudnitzky) (Mobile Movie School anlässlich des 31. Open AirFilmfests Weiterstadt).

References

Appadurai, A. 1996. 'Disjuncture and Difference in the Global Cultural Economy', in *Modernity at Large*. Minneapolis: University of Minnesota Press.

Baker, C., Schleser, M. and Kasia, M. 2009. 'Aesthetics of Mobile Media Art', *Journal of Media Practice*—special issue *A Decade of Media Practice: Changes, Challenges and Choices*—10 2 (3): 119.

Citron, Michelle. 1999. *Home Movies and other Necessary Fictions*. Minneapolis, London: University of Minnesota Press, 1998.

Curtis, Robin. 2006. *Conscientious Viscerality: The Autobiographical Stance in German Film and Video*. Berlin: edn imorde.

Davenport, Thomas and Beck, John. 2002. *The Attention Economy: Understanding the New Currency of Business*. Bosten: Harvard Business Press.

David, G. 2010. 'Camera Phone Images, Videos and Live Streaming: A Contemporary Visual Trend', *Visual Studies*, 25 (1), (April 2010): 89.

Dockney, J. and Thomaselli, K. 2010. 'Third Screens, Third Cinema, Third Worlds and Triadomania: Examining Cellphilm Aesthetics in Visual Culture', *Communitas*: 15 (1).

Frieden, Sandra. 1983. *Autobiography Self Into Form. German Language Autobiographical Writings of the 1970's*. Frankfurt am Main, Bern, New York: Verlag Peter Lang.

Frisch, C. 2007. *Why didn't Anybody Tell me it would become this Bad in Afghanistan*. Netherlands.

Kaganof, A. 2006/7. *SMS Sugar Man*. South Africa.

DOI: 10.1057/9781137469816.0021

Lebow, Alisa. 2012. *The Cinema of Me – The Self and Subjectivity in Fist Person Documentary*. New York: Columbia University Press.

Lejeune, P. 1994. *Der autobiographische Pakt*. Frankfurt am Main: Bayer und Dieter Hornig. Suhrkamp.

Lorenzo, C. 2011. 'The Mobile Aesthetics of Cell Phone Made Films: A short History', *Cinemascope* 17:1 online, www.cinema-scope.com (accessed March 30, 2014).

Matthew, Noel-Tod. 2005. *Nausea* (UK).

Morder, J. 2008. *J'aimerais partager le Printemps avec Quelqu'un*. France.

Pearsall (2013) Online http://www.bbc.co.uk/news/uk-24992393

Rose, J. 2013. *Assembly line Pittance: How Union Agreements are Bypassed (Hungerlohn am Fliessband: Wie Tarife ausgehebelt warden)* Sued-West Deutscher Rundfunk Germany.

Schleser, Max. 2010. 'The Mobile Wave', in *Culture Visuelle*. http://culturevisuelle.org/corazonada/2010/09/11/the-mobile-wave/

Schleser, Max. 2011. *Mobile-Mentary. Mobile Documentaries in the Mediascape*. Saarbrücken, Germany.

Schleser, Max. 2013. 'From "Script to Screen" to "sh%t n share"', in J. Daniels, C. McLaughlin and G. Pearce (eds), *Truth, Dare or Promise—Art and Documentary Revisited*. Newcastle: Cambridge Scholar Publishing.

Schleser, M. and David, G. 2013. 'Mobile AR—Creating Augmented Experiences', in *Anti-po-des Journal of Design Research* 2 (August). www.anti-po-des-designjournal.org.nz/current-issue/abstracts-and-papers/schleser-david/

Schleser, M. 2007. *Max with a Keitai*. Japan/UK.

Smith, S. and Watson, J. (eds) 2001. *Reading Autobiography. A Guide for Interpreting Life Narratives*. Minneapolis, London: Minnesota University Press.

Sobchack in Gaine and Renov (eds) 1999. *Collecting Visible Evidence*. Minneapolis, London: University of Minnesota Press.

DOI: 10.1057/9781137469816.0021

Index

DOI: 10.1057/9781137469816.0022

GPSR Compliance
The European Union's (EU) General Product Safety Regulation (GPSR) is a set
of rules that requires consumer products to be safe and our obligations to
ensure this.

If you have any concerns about our products, you can contact us on

ProductSafety@springernature.com

In case Publisher is established outside the EU, the EU authorized
representative is:

Springer Nature Customer Service Center GmbH
Europaplatz 3
69115 Heidelberg, Germany